The Gloucestershire 11+ Grammar School Handbook

for 2021 Entry

Everything you wanted to know about Gloucestershire Grammar School entrance but were too afraid to ask!

Cotswold
Education
Learning in Community

Published by Fortson Todd Publishing

ISBN: 978-1-912936-03-8

Cheltenham, United Kingdom

Cover photograph: Ian Todd

Foreword

As parents of seven children between us and having spent many years tutoring for the 11+ test, we are only too aware of how time consuming and confusing it can be to go through the process of applying for grammar school. We have accumulated a wealth of useful information and tips. These will help both you and your child prepare, and this increased knowledge of the test, can potentially improve their chances of success.

We have produced this handbook with the aim of putting together all that useful information in one handy volume. There is information on Gloucestershire grammar schools, how to apply, how to appeal against allocations, and how to teach your child the topics in the 11+ exam. We've used jargon free, straightforward language whilst explaining some of the terms and phrases that will help you understand the process.

This is the first edition and we welcome comments and feedback on additional topics you would like to see covered for future years.

We would like to thank all those that have helped in the production of this book including the valuable contributions from discussions with parents and children. We would particularly like to thank Barry Fortson for preparing the content for publication and Sarah Todd and Ellie Todd for comments on early drafts of the text.

We hope you find the handbook a valuable addition to your bookshelf.

Ian Todd & Liz Fortson

March 2020

IMPORTANT INFORMATION RELATED TO THE COVID-19 VIRUS SITUATION

At the time of publication schools are largely closed and public gatherings are not permitted. This means that mock tests and even possibly the actual test may be affected. Please be aware of any announcements regarding changes to secondary school entrance arrangements and look for updates on our Facebook page and website www.cotswoldeducation.co.uk.

Contents

Why Grammar School?

A Brief History of Grammar Schools

Grammar schools have a long history in the UK, with around 1400 existing during their heyday in the early 1960s. However, today there are none remaining in Scotland or Wales and only 160 in England, sporadically distributed between counties. There are also 69 grammar schools in Northern Ireland.

The Old Crypt School Room, Southgate Street, Gloucester

Originally, they were linked to universities or churches, but in the sixteenth century many were established by rich benefactors, paying a Master to teach children Latin and Greek. By the Victorian era the curriculum had broadened to include mathematics and science.

Modern grammar schools are generally recognised as having a more academically focused curriculum with expectations of high performance from their students - the majority moving on to higher education.

Distribution of Grammar Schools

The number of grammar schools has declined rapidly leaving a very patchy distribution remaining throughout England. Some counties have a large number of grammar schools, such as Kent with 32, while others have very few or none at all.

Gloucestershire has a total of seven grammar schools; two co-educational in Cheltenham and Gloucester, three all-girl (two in Gloucester and one in Stroud) and two all-boy in Gloucester and Stroud.

Are Grammar Schools Better?

There is an argument that since grammar schools are selective on academic ability, they are bound to be 'better' academically than comprehensive schools. Whilst there is an element of truth in this statement, the value that schools add to student performance can be argued as the most important way a school can help a child.

Some may argue that comprehensive schools are better resourced and equipped to deal with special needs or other support a child may need since they may have a greater range of student abilities. Comprehensive schools may also have a larger number of students overall and are able to secure funding for more expensive specialist facilities such as drama studios or media centres. However, as grammar schools have increased their intake, they have secured funding to develop particular areas of the curriculum, especially if they have been able to demonstrate an increased number of pupil premium students.

Pros and Cons of Grammar Schools

Every school is different and it can be helpful to research each school as much as possible; an Open Day or Evening will help you get a feeling for the ethos of the school. Usually current students will show you around, giving you and your child a sample of the grammar school environment.

Grammar schools often have excellent examination results, partly because they tend to focus on this aspect of the curriculum. There is often a focus on STEM (Science,

Technology, Engineering and Mathematics) subjects, but that is not necessarily the case for all schools. Some may have a particular focus on languages or music and drama. For more specific information on the Gloucestershire grammar schools please see chapter 2.

This emphasis on academic achievement does not necessarily suit all children. Some may have more practical or vocational interests which are better met at a comprehensive school. However, good comprehensive schools might be a better fit for some children of all academic abilities.

Should I Choose a Grammar School?

There is no definitive answer to this question. Every child is different, and some may be better suited to the grammar school environment than others. Some parents believe that grammar schools are part of an inherently unfair system since there are a disproportionately small number of children from lower income families at most grammar schools. Many parents also believe that tutoring gives a significant advantage to children taking the grammar school entrance test and therefore wealthier parents are more likely to be able to secure a place for their child. However, we would reassure parents that many children succeed in getting into grammar school with little or no tutoring. One of the main purposes of this book is to enable you to prepare your child for the test yourself with minimal additional outlay.

We're assuming that readers of this book have not ruled out the possibility of their child attending grammar school and the ultimate decision on whether to try for grammar schools will be based on a number of factors. These will include assessment of your child's academic ability, the specialisms of a particular grammar school (such as drama, music, languages or science), ease of travel to the grammar school (including costs) and the reputation or performance of your local comprehensive school.

We hope that this book will help you find out more about whether grammar school is for you and your child and to prepare you for this important education decision.

2

Gloucestershire Grammar Schools

Gloucestershire is one of the few English counties that have several selective grammar schools remaining. Of the seven grammar schools, two are coeducational, three are for girls only and two are for boys only. One of these grammar schools is in Cheltenham, four are in Gloucester and two are in Stroud. The following sections give some background information on the school, its academic results and OFSTED ratings.

We have gathered a range of useful information from official figures to help you get an overall impression of the school. However, we suggest that you treat the data with care

and try to view the school as a whole. The school websites are a great starting point as you can get a better impression of the ethos and vision as well as data on examination results and links to the OFSTED reports. You can also find out about recent student achievements and extra-curricular activities.

Open Days are one of the best ways to find out whether your child would be suited to a particular school since you get the opportunity to speak to staff and current students. You may be escorted around the school by a couple of current students, but bear in mind that no one or two students can realistically represent the school population when they are showing you the facilities. They may or may not match the interests and character of your child, but they will have some useful insight into the reality of being a student at that school.

Above all be bold in asking schools the questions you need answering that relate to your child and be realistic on what any one school can provide.

Pates Grammar School

Princess Elizabeth Way, Cheltenham, Gloucestershire, GL51 0HG
Telephone: 01242 523169
Website: https://www.patesgs.org

Awards & Achievements
The Sunday Times State Secondary School of the Year 2020

School Vision
Our school community shares a vision of 'Nurturing Excellence' through 'Embracing Challenge', 'Supporting Each Other' and 'Shaping the Future'.

Progress 8 ranking (KS2 to KS4):	4th within Gloucestershire
Number of pupils:	1100
Number of staff (Full Time Equivalent):	62
Staff Student ratio:	1:17.5
Year 7 intake:	150
OFSTED summary:	Outstanding
GCSE results 2019 (Grades 7-9):	88%
A level results 2019 (Grades B-A*):	96%
Progress from Stage 2 to 4:	0.79
Percentage of free school meal pupils:	2%
Absence (from am/pm sessions):	4%

Pates Grammar School is the only Gloucestershire grammar school based in Cheltenham. It requires a higher score than any of the other grammar schools in Gloucestershire to secure a place here and some students travel long distances.

The school is known for its very good academic record and states that it 'nurtures excellence', but also encourages this in all aspects of student life. The progress score of 0.79 is well above the average for most schools suggested there is a lot of 'value added' to students' academic abilities.

Crypt School

Podsmead Road, Gloucester, GL2 5AE
Telephone: 01452 530291
Website: https://www.cryptschool.org/

School Vision

The vision is underpinned by our five key values of Crypt school life:
Perseverance, Respect, Responsibility, Resilience, Tolerance

Progress 8 ranking (KS2 to KS4):	7th in Gloucestershire
Number of pupils:	1000
Number of staff (Full Time Equivalent):	53
Staff Student ratio:	1:17.8
Year 7 intake:	150
OFSTED summary:	Outstanding
GCSE results (Grades 7-9):	58%
A level results (Grades B-A*):	88%
Progress from Stage 2 to 4:	0.67
Percentage of free school meal pupils:	7.3%
Absence (from am/pm sessions):	3.2%

Crypt is the only co-educational grammar school in Gloucester and prides itself on a reputation as a caring and friendly school.

The School has excellent exam results and students' progress onto university, work-place apprenticeships and employment. There is a focus on pastoral care to encourage students to grow in confidence and instil respect towards others. The careers programme of the school prepares leavers to take their place as valuable members of the community in the wider world.

Denmark Road High School for Girls

Denmark Road, Gloucester, GL1 3JN
Telephone: 01452 543335
Website: https://www.denmarkroad.org

Awards & Achievements

The Sunday Times Southwest State School of the Year 2020

School Vision

We create empowered individuals ready to move forward with confidence, curiosity, integrity and commitment. We, individually and collectively, are ready to discover and realise our personal best, with honour, shaping our futures by creating opportunity and flourishing through challenge and change.

Progress 8 ranking (KS2 to KS4):	1st in Gloucestershire
Number of pupils:	880
Number of staff (Full Time Equivalent):	45
Staff Student ratio:	1:19.8
Year 7 intake:	150
OFSTED summary:	Outstanding
GCSE results (Grades 7-9):	74%
A level results (Grades B-A*):	70%
Progress from Stage 2 to 4:	0.90
Percentage of free school meal pupils:	4.9%
Absence (from am/pm sessions):	4.7%

Denmark Road High School for Girls has an excellent progress record of 0.90 and has a reputation of high academic standards, with GCSE results well above average. In recent years they have achieved success in sports, computing and technology.

The school is currently focussing on developing learners for university and the world of work. There are specific programmes tailored for those looking at careers in medicine and law.

Sir Thomas Rich's

Oakleaze, Longlevens, Gloucester GL2 0LF
Telephone: 01452 338400
Website: https://www.strschool.co.uk

Awards & Achievements

SSAT Educational Outcomes Award by being in the top 10% of schools nationally for progress made by pupils between their key stage 2 results at primary school and their GCSE results at age 16.

School Vision

Sir Thomas Rich's aims to develop students with self-discipline, a thirst for learning, enquiring and creative minds and an appreciation of our heritage. Pride in belonging to this Blue Coat school will ensure that pupils profit from the many opportunities they are offered. They will be well prepared to take responsible places in adult life.

Progress 8 ranking (KS2 to KS4):	5th in Gloucestershire
Number of pupils:	1000
Number of staff (Full Time Equivalent):	55
Staff Student ratio:	1:18.4
Year 7 intake:	150
OFSTED summary:	Outstanding
GCSE results (Grades 8-9):	48%
A level results (Grades B-A*):	74%
Progress from Stage 2 to 4:	0.69
Percentage of free school meal pupils:	4.0%
Absence (from am/pm sessions):	4.6%

Sir Thomas Rich's School in Gloucester is a selective grammar school for boys, with a co-educational sixth form. It has been awarded Specialist College status in three areas (Languages, Science and Leading Edge Mentor School).

The school is proud of its heritage and recognises its sporting achievements. Its current strategy is looking at a number of areas including: improving mental health provision, striving for increased opportunities of learning resources and enhancing opportunities for expressive arts.

Ribston Hall High School

Stroud Rd, Gloucester GL1 5LE
Telephone: 01452 382249
Website: https://www.ribstonhall.gloucs.sch.uk

School Vision
Our ethos is to enable and empower young women to discover their own unique potential. We believe that each child's individuality should be encouraged and developed.

Progress 8 ranking (KS2 to KS4):	11th in Gloucestershire
Number of pupils:	830
Number of staff (Full Time Equivalent):	54
Staff Student ratio:	1:15.6
Year 7 intake:	150
OFSTED summary:	Good
GCSE results (Grades 7-9):	50%
A level results (Grades B-A*):	31%
Progress from Stage 2 to 4:	0.41
Percentage of free school meal pupils:	7.9%
Absence (from am/pm sessions):	4.1%

Ribston Hall has a co-educational sixth form and a strong tradition in music, dance and drama. The current Head is a Biologist and is placing more emphasis on STEM (Science, Technology, Engineering and Maths) subjects, supported by the addition of a new Science block.

The school also strives to provide excellent student wellbeing services, encouraging physical and mental fitness in their students.

Stroud High School for Girls

Beards Lane, Stroud, GL5 4HF
Telephone: 01453 764441
Website: www.stroudhigh.gloucs.sch.uk

School Vision

A learning partnership valuing respect, personal best ... and a spirit of fun

Progress 8 ranking (KS2 to KS4):	2nd in Gloucestershire
Number of pupils:	990
Number of staff (Full Time Equivalent):	48
Staff Student ratio:	1:20.2
Year 7 intake:	150
OFSTED summary:	Outstanding
GCSE results (Grades 7-9):	77%
A level results (Grades B-A*):	80%
Progress from Stage 2 to 4:	0.91
Percentage of free school meal pupils:	4.1%
Absence (from am/pm sessions):	5.7%

The school has invested in a major improvement of its facilities over the past ten years included refurbished and new classrooms, modern ICT facilities including video conferencing facilities, dance studio and kiln room.

The school emphasises the broad range of opportunities available to students included many extra-curricular clubs and societies and links with industry.

Marling School

Cainscross Road, Stroud, GL5 4HE

Telephone: 01453 762251

Website: https://www.marling.gloucs.sch.uk

School Vision

Raising aspirations, inspiring excellence, succeeding together

Progress 8 ranking (KS2 to KS4):	9th in Gloucestershire
Number of pupils:	968
Number of staff (Full Time Equivalent):	52
Staff Student ratio:	1:18.6
Year 7 intake:	150
OFSTED summary:	Outstanding
GCSE results (Grades 7-9):	55%
A level results (Grades B-A*):	69%
Progress from Stage 2 to 4:	0.42
Percentage of free school meal pupils:	3.7%
Absence (from am/pm sessions):	8.0%

The school aims to teach its students to be independent learners and thinkers, taking responsibility for their learning and success and taking an interest in the world around them.

Marling also promotes the five 'British values' defined as democracy, the rule of law, personal responsibility and individual liberty, mutual respect and tolerance of those of different faiths and beliefs as part of the school's approach to learning.

What about Comprehensive Schools?

It is possible to obtain similar data for comprehensive schools but there are many more comprehensive schools in the county, and you are encouraged to do your own research on these.

There are some useful government websites such as http://www.compare-school-performance.service.gov.uk where you can get statistical and numerical information. However, we would always recommend you also look at the school's own website and go along to an Open Day or Open Evening to get a feel for the study environment.

Even if you are sure that you want your child to go to grammar school it is crucial that you put at least once comprehensive school on your school application form and it is recommended that you look at all that your child is eligible to attend, based on catchment areas.

Ultimately your choice will be based on a number of factors, including catchment areas and your child's grammar school test result, which you will receive before you need to submit your school preference application form.

3

The Application and Results Process

Applying for a grammar school in Gloucestershire is a two-stage process. You first register to take the 11+ test and then, after the results are released, apply for your preferred schools in Gloucestershire. It is essential that you send all the information by the relevant deadlines to make the process as stress free as possible.

Do Your Homework

To be as well-informed as possible about all the potential schools you need to do research to decide which schools to consider for your child. Look online, read parents' forums, talk to those that have children in school, read OFSTED reports and visit the school.

Be realistic about your expectations from your child and the school. It is a fact that not all those that apply for grammar school will get a place, so make sure you have a Plan B in place should you need to make alternative arrangements.

Registering to Sit the Grammar School Entrance Test (11+)

If there is any chance at all that you would like your child to go to grammar school in Gloucestershire, you must register them to sit the test. This ensures they will be able to take the 11+ in September with all other children that want to be considered. You can go to the website of any of the Gloucestershire grammar schools to complete the form, either online or in paper format. You do not need to live in Gloucestershire to do this.

Registration for the test is online and opens during June. Our advice is to put all possible grammar schools down on the form which your son or daughter could go to. There is no penalty in putting them all on the list and the few seconds you spend doing this may well be fruitful later on. We have spoken to many parents on results day, wishing they had put one of the 'lower-ranked' schools on their list because they would much prefer that to their local comprehensive school.

The school at the top of your list is the one where you will sit the test, NOT necessarily your preferred school. This registration procedure merely indicates all the schools you want to consider for your child, so the first school in the list can be the grammar school closest to where you live, or is the most convenient for you to visit on the test day. Please note that Pates is often oversubscribed, so if you put them first on your list you may be allocated another school to sit the test. Please note that you score will still be shared with Pates and there is no disadvantage sitting the test at another school.

It is crucial that you complete and submit this form by the deadline (usually the end of June). If you fail to complete the form on time you will need to apply later in the year, (usually around March), and take the test as a late entry Whilst this isn't a disaster, having the test and forms completed sooner rather than later takes a lot of stress out of the application process. It also gives you valuable information before you fill out your school application form, called the Common Application Form (CAF), in October.

Results Day

The results from the entrance test are generally released around three weeks after the test on a Friday. In recent years the schools have been emailing results directly to parents in the morning, leading to a sometimes-nervous day of waiting to tell your child the result when they get back from school.

It's always going to be very nerve-wracking when you open the email to discover the score and rank of your child. It is a good idea to understand in advance what information these emails contain so you are not confused and can identify whether your child is likely to be allocated a place in each of your chosen grammar schools.

Scores and Schools

Each grammar school has 150 places available for Year 7 entry. This brings the total number of places to 1,050, which is a 31% increase from 2012 (800 places). However, the number of children taking the 11+ exam has also been increasing as shown in the table below.

Entry Year	Est. Number Taking the Test
2017	2,150
2018	2,100
2019	2,200
2020	2,500+ (Registered)

When you receive your child's results, you can get a good idea of which school they will qualify for based on the historical record of what ranking has previously resulted in an offer of a place at a particular school. The table below has been collated from information on forums to give an indication of how ranks have changed in recent years. However, these cannot, of course, be an accurate indication of ranks for future years.

Previous Lowest Acceptance Rankings by results year

School	2017	2018	2019
Pates	176	175	175
Sir Thomas Rich's	274	293	293
Denmark Road	325	325	318
The Crypt	803	803	810
Ribston Hall	503	454	550
Stroud	375	436	436
Marling	385	375	340

Considering the Test Results

You should receive the results by email from each of the schools, separately. At this stage you should be in one of four situations:

1. Confident that the rank obtained will get you into your preferred grammar school

2. Unsure about your preferred grammar school, but confident that your child will secure a place at one of the other grammar schools

3. Have qualifying scores but unsure if this is high enough to secure a place at a grammar school.

4. Not have a qualifying score at any of the grammar schools.

You have a number of options depending on which of these situations you are in:

1. If you are in the top 150 rank for your preferred school, make sure you put it top of the list when you apply for schools on the Common Application Form (CAF).

2. If your child has achieved a qualifying score, put your preferred grammar school first, followed by each of the other grammar schools you would like followed by a comprehensive school where you are in the catchment area.

3. Put grammar schools in your order of preference but with the expectation you may have to go to appeal if you are not offered a place. Put your preferred comprehensive school(s) after these.

4. You could consider an appeal, but you should not put grammar schools on the school application form as they will not be taken into account. Put your preferred non grammar schools in order and consider going for an appeal if circumstances allow.

Unless you are very confident of a grammar school place (Option 1 above) you should name a comprehensive school on your form unless you are certain you will choose an independent school if a grammar school place is not available.

If you or your child have attended one of Cotswold Education's events during the academic year leading up to the results you will be offered a free telephone or in person consultation with one or our experienced educational professionals. This will help you understand the consequences of the emails you have received and what you should do next.

Completing the Common Application Form

If you submitted the grammar school entrance test on time you will have the test results from the grammar schools before you fill out the Common Application Form (CAF), but whatever your situation you must complete and submit this form by the deadline, which is usually the end of October, prior to the academic year you are applying for.

It is important to remember that when you fill out the form you are giving your order of preference and therefore technically not choosing which school your child will attend. The distinction may seem minor, but it means that the decision of school allocation is not with the parents. There is simply a preference which will be taken into account when places are allocated.

How to Rank the Schools on the Common Application Form

The CAF allows you to rank up to five schools in order of preference. The GCC Admissions Team will consider your preferences with equal weighting. This is the so-called Equal Preference System. The local authority or school is no longer allowed, by law, to give preference for those that have given a higher rank to a particular school. In many ways this is a good thing, since you don't have to worry that if you haven't put a particular school first you won't be considered.

Places are allocated on how well each student fits the admissions criteria. The text below is taken directly from the Admissions Guidance booklet which explains how the system works in practice:

> On the Common Application Form you will be asked to list your top 5 choices of schools/academies in order of preference. After the closing date, we will put your child's name on the list for each of the schools you have listed. Their position on the list will depend on how well your child fits the school's admission criteria – for example, they may be higher up a school's list if you live very near to it.

> The Equal Preference system means that at this stage, the order in which you ranked the schools will not be taken into account. Your child will be put on the list for every school you have applied to. Each school has a Published Admission Number (PAN): the number of places it has to offer. We will mark up the names at the top of each school's list, up to its PAN. This is known as the School List. Those children whose names fall

outside the PAN will not be offered a place at this school. You will have the opportunity to place your child's name on a waiting list as part of the process for the second stage.

If your child's name appears on only one School List, your child will be offered a place at that school, regardless of where it ranked in your preferences as long as the child falls within the school's PAN (see above).

If your child is on more than one School List, we will then take into account the order in which you ranked the schools on your Common Application Form. Your child will be offered a place at the school that you ranked highest.

If your child isn't allocated a place at any of your preferred schools, we will allocate a place at the nearest school with a space available.

If you have been offered a school that wasn't your first choice, you will then have the opportunity to request for your child to be placed on the waiting list for your higher preferences; so your child may be reconsidered for a place at any of these schools in subsequent allocation rounds.

Source: https://www.gloucestershire.gov.uk/media/2091756/secondary-guidance-booklet-2020.pdf (page 5)

If your school preference is still a grammar school, you must put this first on your form. Then put your preferences in order. Most people will put their other preferred grammar schools next followed by their local comprehensive. It's important to have at least one comprehensive school listed on your form to try and avoid being allocated a school you are not in favour of.

There is no point in listing a grammar school where your child did not reach the qualifying score, as this will not be considered. Note that this does not preclude you from lodging an appeal after Allocation Day, so keep this in reserve, if necessary.

Once you have completed your form remember to submit it! The deadline is the end of October but it's best not to leave it to the last minute. Now you just have to wait for Allocation Day the following March.

Allocation Day

Allocation Day is usually on 1st March (unless it falls on a weekend) and is the day when you hear which school your child has been allocated. If it is the school you had put first on your preference list you just need to accept this place, reject the others and make sure you do this by the deadline, which is generally only a week later.

It is worth repeating the importance of rejecting all the other schools if you have been allocated your preferred school. If you accept your preferred school and ask to go on the waiting list of any other school, you may lose your first choice and be allocated you 'waiting list' school. It may then take a lot of time and effort to be reallocated your preferred choice.

If your allocated school is not your first preference, it's important you take the right steps to maximise your chances of getting your most preferred school. You should **accept** the school offered to you but indicate on the form that you want to go on the waiting list for your most preferred school. This means you will be given a place at this school should a place become available and you fulfil the admissions criteria.

Take care NOT to reject your allocated school since it means you will lose this place and could be allocated another school not on your preference list.

Re- Allocation Day

Your final(ish) school place will be given to you at the end of March after some movement of students between schools based on the responses to Allocation Day. You may have been allocated a comprehensive school and chosen to go on the waiting list for a grammar school. It is possible some children will be removed from the grammar school list as they could move out of the area or choose another school and in this case, you could lose your comprehensive place but be offered your preferred grammar school.

Even if you still have not been allocated your first-choice school you can remain on the waiting list throughout the summer right up until school starts in September. We know of someone who gave up hoping for a grammar school place and bought uniform for their allocated comprehensive school. They were very pleased that they found very late that they had a grammar school place but were left with a set of school uniform to try and dispose of!

Thus, the message is never give up, and even then, a few students will secure places after the year has started or in subsequent school years.

4

The Gloucestershire Grammar School Entrance Test

Most people know the grammar school entrance test as the '11+' which was the term used many years ago for the test which children took to determine if they could secure a place at their local grammar school. The term is rather misleading since it is taken when most children are only ten years old. As we learnt earlier, grammar schools were more numerous in the 1960s and most children had a local grammar school which they could apply for. The tests were generally taken in the child's primary school and they learnt whether they had 'passed' or 'failed' to get into the grammar school. There was no ranking involved and the process was much simpler. However, as fewer grammar schools remained, the process became more complex and in Gloucestershire today there are a number of schools to choose from, all having a different standard of test performance to secure a place.

The Current 11+ Test

Since 2014 the grammar school entrance test for Gloucestershire has been administered using the CEM (Centre for Evaluation & Monitoring), Durham format. This replaced the previous GL assessment and requires a wider range of knowledge and skills.

The stated reason for the change was to make the test more 'tutor proof', as there were concerns that children were being intensively tutored to help them pass the previous GL

test, which was entirely multiple choice 'verbal reasoning'.

The new CEM test was trialled with children that had taken the previous GL test to test for consistency and comparison with scores and ranking. The result of this testing was the introduction of the revised test in September 2014. At the same time the timeframe of test results and application form were revised. Previously the

Common Application Form was completed before the results of the 11+ were known which made ranking schools very difficult. The current system is much more logical, enabling parents to know their child's ranking at each grammar school before applying.

What is the Format of the 11+ Test?

The Gloucestershire Grammar School Entrance Test consists of two test papers, each taking around 50 minutes to complete. Children take the test at the grammar school they have been allocated, in classrooms of about 30 students. Instructions to take the test are played on a CD to ensure all students have exactly the same instructions, regardless of where they take the exam. Each paper consists of a number of different sections that are all timed separately. Once a section has been completed students are not allowed to turn back to finish or change their answers.

Between the first and second paper the children take a refreshment break of about 15 minutes before sitting the second paper under the same examination conditions.

The majority of questions are multiple choice with four or five answers. Some of the maths questions are 'free choice', meaning the children must work out the exact answer and write it on the answer sheet. Children should have the opportunity to familiarise themselves with how to complete the answer sheet which is computer marked. It is therefore important to make sure all answers are clearly marked and any rubbing out of incorrect answers is done thoroughly.

What Types of Questions are in the 11+ Test?

There are broadly four types of question in the Gloucestershire 11+ Test: Comprehension, Verbal Reasoning, Non-Verbal Reasoning and Numerical Reasoning. These are briefly explained below but this guide contains chapters on each type of question to give more detail on what might be included.

- *Comprehension:* A passage of text is provided which may be fiction or nonfiction. The child must read the text and then answer a series of multiple-choice questions based directly on that passage. There is likely to be more than one comprehension section, but this has not been specified.
- *Verbal Reasoning:* These questions are what we might broadly call 'English'. There may be questions on synonyms, antonyms, multiple word meanings, fill in the

missing word, jumbled sentences and others. There is no guarantee that a particular question type has or hasn't come up before so it's important to be prepared with a large range of question types.

- *Non-verbal Reasoning:* These questions focus on shapes, space and patterns which rely less on English or Mathematics ability and more on logic and spatial awareness, among other skills. Some children thrive on these question types whilst others may struggle, but practice always pays dividends in getting to grips with these tasks.

- *Numerical Reasoning:* This is essentially mathematics. There may be question on basic numeracy, probability, timetable problems, money problems, and understanding data presentation. Good mental maths and times tables knowledge are a real asset for these questions and more details are given later in this book.

You may be thinking that this seems like a very wide-ranging test and would be very difficult to pass. Undoubtedly the test is challenging and it would be very hard to score 100%, but the important outcome is how one student compares against the others. More information on ranking and results is given elsewhere in this handbook.

Is The 11+ Test in Gloucestershire Tutor-Proof?

The short answer to this question is no. The long answer is also quite probably no because there is nothing fundamentally different to the previous test, other than it also covers a broader range of question types.

The reasoning behind tutor-proofing the 11+ test was a laudable one -to try and minimise the effect of tuition on the chance of securing a grammar school place. This would give children from families who were unable to afford private education, a better chance of getting into a grammar school.

In reality it is, of course, impossible to devise a test where there is no advantage in preparation. It seems obvious that a child aware of the structure and content of the test is likely to do better than one that arrives on test day with no knowledge of what to expect. It's possible to argue over how much preparation is advantageous, but the Sutton Trust (who strive for social mobility) in their report of 2013 recommended that there should be provision for 'a minimum ten hours test preparation for all pupils to provide a level playing field.'

Source: https://www.suttontrust.com/our-research/poor-grammar-entry-grammar-schools-disadvantaged-pupils-england/

The difficulty is that there is no central funding for this nominal ten hours of tuition, so many children have no real preparation for the 11+ test, while others may have upwards of 100 hours of tuition and preparation. The decision not to tutor may not necessarily be a financial one, but we would recommend some kind of preparation to help your child approach the test with confidence, or at least not with a sense of uncertainty or dread.

Preparing your child doesn't necessarily cost a fortune. You can use short term courses or events in conjunction with mock tests to avoid tuition costs, but you may still need to do some teaching sessions with your child. The next chapter helps you decide whether you'll use a tutor or do it yourself.

5

Do-It-Yourself or Tutoring?

Families are all different, with varying commitments and living in environments which may or may not be conducive to productive learning. The decision of whether to work with your own child, or rely upon a tutor to teach and guide, should be assessed with your particular circumstances in mind.

Some of the reasons that many people choose to pay for tuition include busy schedules, noise from siblings, feelings of being unqualified to offer the help required, potential friction arising between parent and child in regard to academic work and learning that 'everyone else' has a tutor. Being able to objectively judge your own child's academic level and progress can be particularly challenging.

Reasons to 'do it yourself ' are equally valid; often you can save over £1000 by going it alone – a parent knows their child's strengths and weaknesses best, some tutors know little more than parents about the test, and the child may feel less anxiety when not a lot of money is being spent on a tutor. An aspect often overlooked is that parents can spend valuable time with their children that might otherwise be swallowed up in the everyday minutiae of busy lives.

There is no shortage of materials to help you work with your own child, and we will guide you regarding relevant ones to choose at different stages of preparation. The best news is that the 11+ is probably not as hard as you might think. National news outlets appear to suggest that most parents probably couldn't pass the test themselves, let alone help their child prepare. By collating some of the most difficult questions and presenting them as typical of the 11+ test, many parents are put off before they even start, and sadly, some suspect their child could not pass based on this information alone and decide not to enter them.

What is clear is that this test is not 'tutor proof', and it would be unwise to expect even the brightest child to gain a place without some time being spent teaching them about what is involved.

By addressing the concerns that the DIY route poses and explaining how you can help your child with their preparation by using this book, we believe they can gain fair access to a grammar school with or without private tuition.

Before you decide whether to 'go it alone' or use a tutor, investigate and make decisions regarding the issues mentioned next as thoroughly as possible.

Planning – Suitability for Grammar School

One of the most commonly asked questions by parents early on in the process is 'How do I know if my child has the academic potential to gain a grammar school place?'. This is not an easy question to answer but there are a number of sources that might help you decided whether to take the process forward.

The Opinion of a tutor

Many parents turn to tutors to answer this question, yet for many tutors it is difficult to assess; knowing the child and making this judgement in a very short time may be unrealistic. Most tutors genuinely wish to offer help to as many children as possible and know that huge academic gains can be made in one school year. They are loathed to deny any child tuition that has what they believe to be, a reasonable chance of success. Other tutors may only accept children that are clearly 'high fliers' (and may need little tuition to pass) in order that the percentage of children they take on and proceed to gain places is very high - thus they appear to be excellent at their job. Therefore, the success rate of a tutor is not necessarily a reliable indication of their ability. Tutors can however gain an excellent reputation, and this is most easily discovered through word-of-mouth, and to some extent on-line reviews. A few tutors will accept almost all children, but hopefully inform parents of their opinion of the likely outcome as soon as this becomes apparent.

The Opinion of My Child's Current Teacher

This discussion may be quite difficult. Some teachers do not believe in the grammar school system and would therefore prefer not to be involved. Also, the teacher may have only known your child for a few weeks when you ask if you think grammar school might suit them, and so would be unable to offer you a clear picture. In this case, it may be appropriate to ask the teacher from their previous school year.

CATs scores - Cognitive Ability Tests

These are Cognitive Ability Tests that children take in the early part of Year 5 in many Gloucestershire primary schools. You may or may not be aware that your child has taken them, and results are not generally offered to the parents unless they are asked for.

However, you may ask for these, and they can be a very good indicator of academic potential. The tests, usually taken over several days and covering verbal, non-verbal and quantitative (numerical) reasoning, may also be very helpful in regard to Grammar School Appeals, see Chapter 12.

Year 2 SATS

Although these are long past, achievement of level 3+ in one or more areas would suggest that a child has worked at a higher academic level than most of their peers at a point in time.

Placement Tests

Aside from assessments made by tutoring establishments, a number of publishers provide 11+ placement tests that provide an assessment of your child's ability. These are designed to identify particular areas of strength and weakness that you are able to address by tutoring or further learning sessions. Cotswold Education provides these types of tests with honest and informative feedback.

Mock Tests

Professionally run Mock Tests are carried out under examination conditions and as well as giving experience of examination conditions can also give a detailed assessment of your child's ranking and areas for development. Chapter 10 gives more detail about these kinds of assessment.

Music Examinations

If your child has had the opportunity to play a musical instrument and reach a high standard, these may be used as an indicator of academic potential. (These may also be considered during an appeal. See Chapter 12.)

School Reports

Recent school reports may indicate progress and highlight your child's academic strengths and weaknesses.

Considering the Evidence

Once you have formed a picture using as much of the evidence as possible, it is time to look further into whether this route is really suitable for your child from an academic stand-point.

We have heard some parents suggest that they will manage if their child is struggling academically once at grammar school by using subject tutors. This might be and probably is possible for one or two subjects, but if it seems likely that more help will be required, we strongly recommend that you reconsider the grammar school option. It is tempting to believe that 'if only my child can get into a certain school' all will be well, but struggling academically in an ill-suited school, can severely damage self-esteem.

Motivation

Is my child self-motivated? Can I help motivate them? Should I rely upon a tutor to do this?

Motivating your child to do work beyond that expected by school can prove challenging. It is probably the number one reason that people rely upon tutors as children are usually more inclined to do extra work that a relative stranger asks of them rather than their own parent! However, it is important to be aware that tutors will also expect work to be done at home. This is why it should not be assumed that preparation will be plain-sailing if left to a tutor.

To enable preparation to run smoothly consider the following:

Does my child want to go to grammar school?

Before answering this, we must consider that most children aged 9, have no clear understanding about what a grammar school is, let alone whether they would really like to attend one. It is only by seeing a grammar school that your child will have a picture in their mind of what they are working towards. Perhaps you are keen for your child to take the 11+ but your child is not. In this case it will be necessary to understand their reasoning and reach a decision together. Perhaps they are concerned about their abilities or wish to avoid peer pressure. Sometimes a compromise can help. The 11+ materials, apart from non-verbal reasoning, are suitable for improving school performance in key subjects namely English and Maths; maybe you can just see how it goes and make decisions later?

Visiting the grammar school Open Days is very important but try not to make all the visits over just a few days. By spreading these days out over the year, you can revive your child's determination to do well. If possible, allow your child the opportunity to speak with some children already attending the grammar school in question. This can provide interesting insights to both you and your child.

A Positive Approach

We suggest that you try not to approach your child with the argument that they should do extra work in order to gain a place at a certain grammar school. Instead present the option of doing a little extra work to increase their chances of having a number of different schools to pick from when they finally come to making such decisions with you. Explain that the work will definitely mean that they are better placed to do well in Year 6 and beyond.

Rather than offering a reward for passing the 11+ we recommend that children are praised for all their hard work before the test itself and you may like to offer small incentives along the way. We would reward attitude and effort, not the result. In the case of my family, I did not provide material incentives along the way, but did write them each a letter the night before the test assuring them that I was very proud of all their hard work and of them as a person; making it clear that the result would make no difference as to who they are or how we would regard them. Before the test it can also be worth discussing numerous highly successful people that supposedly 'failed' the test.

Timing - when to begin preparation

Try not to be tempted to start 11+ workbooks or tuition too soon. If you wish to begin preparing your child for the exam before Year 5, we strongly advise you to play maths, language and logic games, reading with your child every day, and help them to learn their multiplication tables 'inside out'. Doing the same style of extra workbook work, as advocated by numerous publishers (that have financial gain in mind), is we believe, likely to be detrimental, with the child often losing interest when they need to be most engaged. If a child needs more than one year of dedicated 11+ preparation in order to pass, this suggests that they are likely to struggle upon arrival even if they pass the test.

Just attempting a few practice papers, a couple of weeks before the exam, is better than no preparation. Familiarisation with the test layout, the type of question likely to be asked, and experience completing an answer sheet, can all have some impact. Many children begin preparation approximately one year before the test, and considering the competitive nature of the 11+, it is probably a good idea to begin then. For some though, this period of preparation is still too long; they 'peak' too soon and become frustrated with the monotony of the question types. Those that begin later should not feel disadvantaged by doing so; it is simply a different approach whereby they may wish to practise a little more each week.

How Much Time Should Be Devoted to DIY 11+ Preparation?

One hour with an adult, and another for the child to work alone should suffice per week, perhaps with 10-minute vocabulary learning sessions before or after school most days. We would also recommend that time is set aside to regularly play games, either over a weekend or one evening a week. If you plan to go it alone with preparation, it is important that you have scheduled times with your child, just as you would if using a tutor. However, from time to time, the obstacles of everyday life will most likely conflict with the timetable that you put in place. Therefore, it is essential that any plan drawn up, and agreed upon with your child, is realistic and provides flexibility. Try to be strict and keep to working at the set times each week, but also have reserve time slots for when needed.

It is tempting for a parent to feel that they are too busy to fit in this extra work themselves, and that may be true. However, we suggest you bear in mind that meeting with a tutor each week is also a time commitment - one that will probably require a journey, finding parking, and time to speak with the tutor yourself. Homework requirements from tutors vary, but you are likely to be expected to help your child with some exercises set.

As mentioned, children usually embark upon their 11+ preparation journey about one year before the test and most are initially very keen. It is as the months wear on, and days get shorter that the grim reality of extra work can lead to friction between parent and child. At such times there is no harm in giving both yourself and your child the odd 'week off', or in doing things differently. Focusing again on word games such as crosswords, hangman and word searches, challenging them to name 10 or more types of bird, tree, fish, home etc, having a go at a mathematical scavenger hunt, or simply playing cards are all great preparation activities. *The Big 11+ Vocabulary Playbook* and *The Big 11+ Logic Puzzle Challenge* provide a wide range of activities to keep the mind working whilst having fun.

We suggest that you leave practice tests until at least the Spring Term before the exam, and even during the summer holiday rarely expect your child to complete two papers in order to finish one whole test at home. There is value in your child attempting two 45/50-minute papers with a 15-minute break between as it may improve stamina. However, preparation for the length of the whole 11+ experience is more successfully accomplished by attending a few 11+ Mock Examinations.

In Chapter 13 (Resources), we provide a list of various practice papers that we have used with children, together with the schools, children have gained places at with certain ranges of practice scores. Practice Paper publishers offer their own suggestions as to the likely success rate of varying scores, however we have found these to state higher scores generally than our experience in Gloucestershire suggests.

When to End Preparation?

Just as importantly as deciding when to begin preparation is knowing when 'enough is enough'. There will come a point when your child will gain more from knowing that you feel confident in their abilities than they will from another practice paper or new vocabulary. As a tutor I always suggest that all 11+ materials are put away about a week before the test. Certainly, no practice papers should be used at this point; a disappointing score could negatively impact confidence and performance on the actual test day.

Marking

In our experience, the hardest part of 11+ preparation from a personal stand point has been marking my own child's practice work and tests. I found it very difficult to remain objective when coming across their 'silly' mistakes. What I needed to keep in mind was that these mistakes rarely were truly silly, but actually an indication that the depth of knowledge of a topic required was not complete. It can be a struggle not to see our children's successes and mistakes as reflections of ourselves. If we can be more objective in our approach, the child can learn unimpeded by our expectations.

From a practical standpoint, the only reasons to mark work are to find areas for improvement, and measure success. Using 11+ materials not specifically designed as tests, I often introduce a topic and then work with the child using alternate questions on a page. Questions that we have not completed together are answered by the child independently. This ensures that what the child attempts independently will be of a level that we have approached together first. When marking practice exercises, I mark correct answers with a tick, and incorrect ones with a dot. I then visit incorrect answers with the child, and we discuss together where the mistake was made. Sometimes I ask a child to self-correct first. If numerous mistakes are being made whilst covering a certain topic, it may well be necessary to take several steps back before moving on. It is also useful to revisit topics regularly.

Am I, the Adult, Clever Enough to Teach my Child for the 11+?

It is OK for you not to know the answers to all the 11+ questions yourself. Working out some answers together, and having your child reach the answer first, will increase their confidence, and by explaining to you how they have reached an answer they are consolidating their own knowledge. It is a brilliant way for them to learn!

The Working Environment

Finding the right working environment can be daunting if you live in a smaller home, and/or have other noise distractions. However, nobody has said that practice must take place in the home. Noah, aged 10, had two younger siblings when preparing for this test, his parents were working, and they were in the middle of moving house. His mother overcame the problem by sitting with him at a table in a quiet area of a sports centre. Alternatives are local libraries or even quiet coffee shops. What is necessary is a peaceful space, and as importantly, setting regular times to work.

It is not necessarily an advantage to always work in a totally quiet space, devoid of any and all distractions. Learning to cope with a minimal degree of background 'noise', could be useful both in the test and at home. We have recently heard reports of carnival music being heard during the 2019 test, with windows open as it was a warm day. Those children that were able to remain focused, would have been at an advantage in this instance.

Handling the Pressure!

Without doubt, taking any test puts pressure upon most participants. In this case, relatively young children are being asked to perform in a strange environment under unfamiliar conditions. This test-taking environment will be very different from any your child has encountered at school. To alleviate some of this pressure is the primary role of mock tests.

It is also essential that each child has a reason not to be unduly worried about the result. This is best achieved by parents portraying positive messages about other school options, whatever their personal feelings. Examples may be given of how older pupils have achieved brilliantly at non-grammar schools, the enjoyment of joining a school with many familiar faces from their primary school, or fantastic facilities. Most importantly the grammar schools themselves are keen for your child to know that if a child does not gain a place, it is not because they have failed, but just that on a particular day they did not achieve a passing score. It is not an indication of lack of intelligence. Knowing that there is an element of 'luck on the day' must always be kept in mind.

Resources

A good tutor will be able to guide you towards buying the correct resources for the programme of study that they intend to use with your child. If you decide to teach yourself, we have listed good resources in Chapter 13.

When buying any 11+ specific resources always be sure that they clearly state they are intended for the CEM 11+ exam, and that any practice papers are also multiple choice (not standard format). There are many publications on the market, and we recommend that you buy them incrementally as needed. Publishers are constantly changing titles and designs of their materials and a visit either to a local book store or online can be baffling. Be aware that CEM (Centre of Education and Monitoring) University of Durham, does not publish practice papers or resources for the test (although they do provide a little in the way of sample materials).

There are books on the market that indicate their suitability for children as young as 7 or 8, but we feel that this is far too soon as your child will see more than enough 11+ material during Year 5 without making the process even longer.

Distance

Whilst it might be tempting to apply for a school a long way from home due it its record of academic success, the potential pitfalls should be addressed. Committing your family to long daily commutes for five or seven years, is a big decision. It may appear relatively simple to rely upon a school bus but any time your child has extra-curricular events or illness, or you need to visit for one reason or another, the distance can be an issue. With friendships being built between children living up to 50 miles apart, it can be hard for children, and reliance upon social media to keep these friendships 'active' can perhaps become a problem too.

Sibling Issues

If you are in the situation of having more than one secondary aged child at one time it may be an advantage for each of them to have some 'space' from their siblings to grow as an individual, or it may simply be personal choice. However, generally speaking the pros of siblings being together outweigh the cons. Convenience, increased knowledge on the parents' part about how a school works, and the comfort for a younger sibling upon joining their elder in a school they already know a little about, can be a real bonus. A separate sibling issue if you have an older child already attending a grammar school is that it can place undue pressure on the younger sibling to achieve too. Our experience is that the issue must be handled delicately but with honesty, encouraging the younger child to feel confident in themselves. Be aware that although you might be managing the situation well at home, outside influences may come into play such as playground chatter. With two older brothers at Pates, my daughter often encountered "You'll obviously want to go to Pates" which only added to the stress of taking the 11+ test.

Before I Begin Checklist

It is useful to start by objectively, honestly and realistically assessing the factors which may impact your decisions.

Things to consider are:

- I am aware of my child's strengths and weaknesses. Is success a realistic probability?
- How will I be able to motivate my child with or without a tutor if things get difficult?
- Where will I work with my child? Where will they work alone?
- Do I have the time?
- What resources do I need?
- Is the distance to school reasonable?
- Will the schools of any siblings make a difference to school choice?

Special Educational Needs

We are unable to tell you exactly what support might be available for your child, but there are a variety of accommodations that are utilised depending upon individual need. Typically, these may include:

- Taking the exam in a room with fewer children

- Any necessary accommodations for physical needs - seating/table arrangement etc

- Overlays for dyslexia

- Possibly a scribe (unlikely due to the nature of the test)

- Possibly rest breaks

- Possibly extra time (up to 25%)

- Auditory/Visual Assistance

Evidence: You must apply for any particular special accommodations when registering for the exam in June.

Acceptable Evidence: Medical Reports with defined diagnosis from a qualified practitioner. Reports from professionals that work at least in part within the NHS are considered preferable to those from elsewhere, however highly qualified the practitioner may be.

Students with Special Education Needs (SEN) may also have an Education, Health and Care Plan (EHCP) which looks more broadly at aspirations, needs and outcomes and identifies additional support which may be needed. This can be important in ensuring special arrangements have been made for the Test.

Consider Applying for Support

We cannot guarantee that supplying the above information ensures your child receive the support that you believe they may be entitled to. Instead, we suggest that you telephone or email Admissions at the grammar schools, particularly the one where you would like your child to sit the exam. The Admissions Officer can offer your clear insight regarding what the school can provide if adequate evidence of need is provided.

6

Elements of the Exam: Verbal Reasoning

You can expect to find a variety of types of verbal reasoning within the two test papers. These are used to assess comprehension skills, word recognition including finding synonyms (similar) and antonyms (opposites) of words, spelling, and to a lesser extent grammar. For a previous type of 11+ tests used by Gloucester before 2013, many children would learn many long lists of words and their meanings. Although such rote learning has its place, it is less helpful today as greater depth in the understanding of language is required.

Vocabulary Tips: Word Recognition

It can be much easier to solve verbal reasoning tasks if you have some new word knowledge. It means you can at least eliminate some of the possible answers to increase the probability of choosing the right answer.

There is a list of words which are likely to be used in the 11+ test at the back of this book which you may find helpful. This list is huge, and we would not expect any child to learn all of these. However, encouraging them to use some of the words and by creating flashcards that are new to your child, can help improve their vocabulary in a relatively short time. When your child has learnt a new word, we strongly encourage them to use it as often as possible. Challenge your child to put it into their school writing at some point in the week that they learn it.

Root Words

It is virtually inevitable that your child will not immediately recognise every word that they come across when practising or taking the 11+. However, with much of English based upon ancient Greek and Latin, knowing root words can be a very useful tool. Knowing the root words below can enable either partial or complete recognition of many new words.

Audio - hear	Ben - good	Logo - word or reason
Chromo - colour	Photo - light	Scope – target/see
Mal - bad	Post - after	Sub - under
Phone - voice/sound	Super -extra	Aqua - water
Poly - many	Bio - life	Mono - one
Geo - earth	Ante - before	Syn - same

Encourage your child to learn these and find as many words as possible that begin with the same letters.

Synonym and Antonym Questions

Often the test asks children to provide a synonym (most similar) or antonym (most opposite) for a particular word from a list of four or five choices. To do this accurately they should consider the following:

- What type of word are they trying to match? If the first word is a noun, the answer must also be a noun. Perhaps it is an adverb, adjective, verb, or preposition?
- Is the initial word positive or negative? The root terms 'mal' signifying 'bad' or 'ben' suggesting 'good' might help here.
- Sometimes within a list where a synonym is being asked for, an antonym is given or vice versa.

    Example: pick a synonym for 'glad' from the words below

    coy   fragile   disappointed   pleased   hexagonal

    Although 'glad' and 'disappointed' are clearly related, they are not synonyms, but it is easy to confuse the two, especially under test conditions.

- Does the word that you think matches the first' word, flow in a sentence in the same way? If your choice of answer is correct, it will work grammatically.
- Never pick a word because it is 'the hardest'. Children often assume that because the 11+ test is considered difficult, then they should pick a word that they don't

recognise! This rarely works. Show your child that they should only do this if they are absolutely certain that no other answer fits.

- Encourage them to be careful and not to be swayed by word connections. The words bucket and spade are often connected but they are not synonyms or antonyms of one another.

Homonyms and Synonyms

Be aware of these special word types as they can easily lead to confusion or an avoidable mistake. It is important to look carefully for these types of word in questions.

Homonyms

These have the same sound but can have the same OR different spelling

Example: fair (Summer fair), fair (reasonable), fare (payment)

Homophones

These always have the same sound but different spellings

Example. fair (Summer fair), fare (payment)

Homographs

These have the same or different sound but with the same spelling

Example. tear (from crying)   tear (rip up)

spoke (part of a wheel)   spoke (speaking in the past tense)

It is not necessary for you to know the grammatical terms for all of these, although you child may have learnt them at school. However, do draw your child's attention to them, as they are easy to miss.

Odd One(s) Out

This question type usually requires the child to identify one of the words that does not fit with the others on the list

Example: toaster   oven   cutting board   microwave

Looking for an odd one or two words out, the child should try to group words that they know first, and then apply knowledge of word types as mentioned above to make their best estimation. In the example above cutting board is the odd one out because the others are used to heat food.

Jumbled Sentences

These questions prove particularly challenging for most children - and adults! There are things that can make them a little easier. Usually a sentence is given with the words jumbled and an extra word added. It is the child's job to sort out the sentence and find the extra word.

Example: waves the sunk boat the huge battered over crashed

Answer: The huge waves crashed over the battered boat. The extra word that is the answer is 'sunk'.

Many children find these questions very time consuming and it can be best to attempt questions that clearly have fewer words first.

Ask your child to always read the sentence in its jumbled form first in order to get a picture of what the sentence is about. What is the subject and object of the sentence? Look for phrases that hang together and try to fit in any adjectives and adverbs as they progress. They must also be aware of homonyms and recognise that the extra word, the answer, can quite easily detract the reader from the meaning of the sentence. Sometimes the sentence may have opposite words such as morning/evening and therefore it is likely that one of these may be the 'extra' word.

Tips for Jumbled Sentences

1. Ask your child to find groups of words that appear to naturally fit together such as 'began to rain'

2. If your child in the exam is told not to write on their question paper, they can quickly write out the sentence on scrap paper provided, and cross with a diagonal (/) line as they work through the word order. If the sentence is not working for them, they can then try again by creating an 'X', and if they have time and are still stuck, circle or underline the words. However due to time limitations we do not suggest they make more than two attempts before moving on to other questions.

3. Your child should attempt shorter sentences first. The task can be very time consuming and shorter sentences are usually a little easier.

4. Sometimes they can estimate that one of two words is likely to be the extra word without ever needing to build the entire sentence. These are often opposites such as 'night' and 'day'.

5. The questions can sometimes take children on a 'wild goose chase' as they try to include misleading words presuming will be part of the answer, ask them to beware of this.

6. This will be a multiple-choice exercise. Perhaps looking at these choices will guide you

7. Try to fit in any 'small' words as you go, for instance adding in adjectives or adverbs.

Cloze Tasks

This is a term used to describe three types of question that may be asked in this test. Certain parts of texts have been removed, and the child must try to work out what is missing.

Type A: Missing words

Sentences or whole passages will be presented with whole words missing. Use the following tricks to help with these:

1. The child will need to draw conclusions through understanding the text so care with reading is required.
2. They may use the multiple-choice answer sheet to help and can use grammatical cues to support their answer.
3. A word bank may be provided and, in this case, they may check what words they have used. However, it is better to put an answer choice twice if they believe it fits, than miss one right answer by avoiding doing this.

Type B: Missing letters

From a word that is part of a sentence (Example: There is p_ _n_y of room)

From a word that is a synonym or antonym of another word. (Example: warm _ hil_ _)

Find the correct three letters to complete the word in capitals

Example: Last Sunday the first daf _ _ _ils of Spring were to be seen

        SOL   CAP   FOD   SKI   BOW

1. We highly recommend that your child has lots of practice with crossword puzzles, these are very similar to what is being asked for here but the format is hopefully more fun.
2. If your child struggles with spelling, these questions will prove very challenging. We recommend *The Survival Guide for Seriously Slippery Spellings* for helping to learn some of the most often misspelled words in English; also, word searches and regular reading.
3. Use letters that are given in the word to provide clues. Some letters are never written together, such as cd or fb, whilst others are regular blends, such as 'ing' or 'spr'.
4. Double letters are often tricky to deal with, and extra should be care taken when these are involved

Type C: Pick the word from a small selection

Children often score quite high marks with these exercises as they appear relatively simple compared with other cloze types. The child though must be careful of grammar usage, spelling and contextual clues.

Example: Calligraphy requires a _____ hand.

pen, parchment, steady, right

Deductive Reasoning - Logic Questions

This is an opportunity to have some fun while doing verbal reasoning tasks. There are many games and activities that will help your child achieve higher marks in a wide range of 11+ questions.

Some recommended games and resources that we've found invaluable are:

- Hang Man
- Bananagrams R
- Word Searches – *The 11+ Word Search Extravaganza*
- Scrabble
- *The Big 11+ Vocabulary Play Book*
- Anagrams

- Crosswords
- Categories
- Twenty Questions

General Verbal Reasoning Tips for your Child

Use these in conjunction with exam technique tips

- Look out for words that sound positive or negative, even if you are not sure of their meanings

- Be sure to be looking for the right type of word i.e. a synonym of an adjective, must be an adjective

- Avoid being distracted by difficult or 'stand-out' words

- Occasionally capital letters may help

- Many of the questions will have two likely answers. Now look very carefully for which of those two is most likely

- Beware of double letters, especially with cloze spelling questions - write out the word if needed

- Beware of homonyms and homophones

- Beware of deliberate mis-spellings

- Beware that if you are looking for synonyms or antonyms that you do not accidentally pick a word that is a connection instead.

7

Elements of the Exam: Comprehension

It is likely that your child is already reading with a reasonable level of competency and that bedtime stories are a thing of the past. Your child has become an independent reader... Hooray!

Unfortunately, this is where comprehension exercises can come as a bit of a shock to many parents. It may well be that your child has come to rely upon contextual cues (an excellent skill in itself), alongside their phonetic knowledge, to follow texts, leading to words silently being misinterpreted. Gaps in knowledge may show themselves when your child reads aloud, between what you have assumed they know, and what they actually do.

An example here is the word 'comprehension'. Children by Year 5 have been doing and using the term 'comprehension' for a long time, yet in all our years of tutoring we have yet to meet a child that knew the verb 'to comprehend' means 'to understand'.

The good news is that of course, with experience, your child will recognise their mistakes and their vocabulary will improve, but that takes time. Therefore, it is important that you once again find time to hear your child read aloud – not necessarily whole books, but at least the comprehension passages that they are working on. It can become clear, not just when the child becomes 'stuck' on words, but also by their misuse of intonation, grammar, and even missing whole lines out, that understanding is lacking.

What to Read

It is important that your child reads literature - books and magazines, from as wide a variety of genres as possible. Encourage them, if you can, to avoid book series for a while, as in terms of language development they provide 'more of the same' in most cases. However, just about any reading is better than no reading and enjoyment is always key.

We recommend, amongst other reading choices, one of the below each month.

If a particular genre is not to your child's taste, do not 'flog a dead book'. However, if they can cover as many genres as possible, it will optimise chances of exploration and discovery through literature and improve reading skills.

Some suggested genres are:

- Biography
- Autobiography
- Science fiction
- Historical fiction/Classics
- Adventure
- Poetry
- A Play
- Informational book on a variety of topics
- Mystery
- Children's newspaper
- Realistic fiction
- Myths/Legends

An extensive list of suitable books is available at www.cotswoldeducation.co.uk and in Chapter 13.

What is the Author Trying to Say? Why?

At the core of all comprehension exercises, is whether the reader has understood the 'main idea' of the text. If this is understood, then most other answers can fall into place, as they relate in some way to this central theme. For your child to become well practised in recognising the main idea, always ask, even if they are not set questions, "What is the author trying to let you know?", and "Why does the author want you to understand this?"

Reading Between the Lines

As your child reads, are they able to discover inferred meanings between the lines of text? The grammar schools want to be able to differentiate between candidates that can read, understand and retrieve information in a basic way, and those that can also use clues in a text to make inferences. This is challenging and requires the child to be aware that not all answers will be directly 'searchable'; they will need to think logically using the information given to discern the unknown. Many children will find this difficult, particularly in a test situation. There is comfort in being able to find a direct answer, and inference questions can leave the child feeling uneasy. It can be useful to ask your child to create their own 'between the lines' question for you to answer about a particular passage, to help them become more prepared for this question type.

Title

Ensure that you always discuss the title of a passage and note if any particular dates are noted in the passage or at the end of the piece. These can give the reader very useful clues with which to identify the passage's meaning, purpose and from what period the passage is set

Vocabulary Book

Discussed in detail in the Vocabulary Section, it is also helpful for your child to have an exercise book on hand at all times, to jot down unfamiliar words and their meanings. This includes words discovered during comprehension exercises and regular reading. Each time they should write the new word, use a dictionary to find its definition, and where appropriate provide at least one antonym.

Speed

Contrary to popular belief the 11+ exam does not have a speed-reading component, and this fact is a second reason for our 'read aloud' mantra. Many children learn in the playground about the 'speed' of the CEM 11+ test, and so it is very understandable that they feel they must read 'super-fast' in order to answer all the questions in the time allowed.

In reality, unless your child is a particularly slow reader, a regular pace is absolutely fine. They should learn to trust in themselves that reading at a natural speed is adequate. By reading together, you can insist that they slow down if rushing to get ahead.

Paragraph by Paragraph

As your child tackles a comprehension passage, we suggest that they check their understanding of each paragraph as they read. Rushing ahead, which can be tempting, will usually make future understanding more difficult.

When Not to Read Aloud

The most obvious answers here are, whilst your child is doing the exam or practice papers, and during mock tests. However, make sure your child is aware that for this test at least, it is not important to pronounce names of people are places correctly, as long as they are able to follow what is going on themselves. Similarly, they need not read out particular large numbers.

When My Child Knows Too Much (or Too Little)

Scenario A: Child with parent beginning a new comprehension piece.

"The text is about the Great Fire of London. Brilliant! I know all about the Great Fire of London" they say.

They proceed to read the text, regularly complaining "they got that wrong" and explaining 'what really happened'. Not only that, the child uses their own knowledge rather than the text's information to answer the questions.

Scenario B: Another new comprehension passage for the child to consider.

"It's all about ballet. That's not fair, I don't know anything about ballet and my friends will"

These situations are examples of how knowledge of a topic related to a text, or lack thereof, can have a negative impact upon the child's approach. In the first case, the child's exuberance upon coming across a topic about which they feel confident, can lead to placing their own understanding of a subject before considering what the author is attempting to express. It is important that the child learns to focus purely on what is in front of them, and not cloud their judgement with information from elsewhere.

The second scenario presents us with the child that feels disadvantaged, and this feeling of despondency may prove costly. It is worth explaining that all they need to know will be in front of them and their presumed disadvantage can actually work in their favour, as reflected by scenario A.

Questions Before Text?

Some tutors recommend that the child looks through the questions before they read the actual text; the advantage being that the questions will give clues about the text, making it easier to read, and then correct answers can be picked out more easily. Our experience is that this is usually not the best way to approach comprehension. We find it can detract from the child's understanding of central themes, and it better to discover the passage as a whole, referring back to particular paragraphs as needed. However, we suggest that you trial both methods and talk with your child to determine what works best for them.

Every Word Counts

It is worth mentioning to your child that printing is expensive! We find this an easy way to explain to children that authors, and poets in particular, are very careful about every single word they write. That being the case, it is worth considering why the words chosen, have been, and so they must be careful not to accidentally miss words when reading.

Character Tracker

Keeping track of which character is doing what, can be quite complicated. Regularly ask your child to pick out the actions of one particular character followed by another, when there are multiple characters to follow.

To Underline or Not, that is the Question?

At this age, your children are likely to be taught in school the importance of under-lining key points whilst attempting comprehension tasks. This is a key skill, wherein they are learning to logically recognise the most significant points in a passage. However, these children are still young, and the skill of under-lining relatively new. In reality, even many students of GCSE age are only just beginning to correctly under-line in this way. Instead, it is likely that the younger child, who is just learning the skill, will spend much time and effort under-lining unnecessary parts. These may even detract from the true answer for which the reader is searching. Instead, we suggest that for a particularly long passage, when marking on the test paper is allowed, they can write a couple of words in the margin to remind them of paragraphs' key themes, and perhaps they might choose to underline dates and numbers only.

Alternative Forms of Writing

It is tempting to expect 11+ comprehension passages to involve literature - fiction or non-fiction. However, there is no reason why the examiners may not ask the candidate to read an instruction manual, advertisement or even a map. Encourage your child to read these through their everyday experiences.

Key Terms in Comprehension

It is important that your child is familiar with the following terms and can recognise their uses in literature.

Metaphor - says something IS something else

Simile - describes something as LIKE something else; often using 'as' or 'like'

Proverb - an old and often wise saying

Personification - giving something not human, human characteristics

Adjective - describes a noun

Adverb - describes a verb

Pronoun - used in place of a noun (e.g. he/she/it/they)

Common noun - non-specific name (e.g. fish/house/field)

Proper noun - a specific name (e.g. London/Pierre)

Collective noun - a group name (e.g. gaggle/batch/herd)

Onomatopoeia - words used for sounds

Alliteration - several words with the same initial sound put together

Irony - a statement with a twist, often stating the opposite of what is actually meant

Preposition - a positioning word for time and place (e.g. under, before, on)

Conjunction - a word used to connect sentences/clauses or to co-ordinate words in the same clause

Cliché - an overused statement, that lacks original thought

Allusion - an expression used to call something to mind, without actually stating what that something is

Analogy - a comparison

Abbreviation - shortened forms of words i.e. etc./Mrs/

Command - a statement telling that something should be done

Homophone - two or more words with different meanings but sound the same (e.g. write and right)

Synonym - words with very similar meanings

Antonym - words with very opposite meanings

Comprehension Tips for Your Child

Use these in conjunction with exam technique tips:

- Avoid picking a humorous answer choice unless you are certain it is correct

- Always look for the very best answer. When there are five possibilities, it is likely that two are quite obviously wrong, another quite unlikely to be correct, and two that at first glance, may appear to be plausible answers. Picking between the 'top two' usually requires extra consideration.

- Focus on what the question is asking; answer choices may well have information from the text but be incorrect in terms of the question being asked

- Never leave an answer blank - make a best guess

- If asked to define a specific word from the text, be sure to look at the words before and after it. Only one meaning of the word will make sense in the context of the passage.

- Be aware of the multiple meanings of many words

- If your child becomes confused whilst reading, remind them not to 'plough through'. After the first few sentences, as soon as the passage is not making sense, try to relax and take a moment to consider what has been said so far. If necessary, re-read.

Comprehension Example

Read the following passage and then answer the questions on the following pages.

I lay on my back in the long grass watching the white clouds swirling and making shapes in the azure sky. The sun was pleasantly warm and all I could hear was the sound of bird song, the rushing stream that wound its way through the grassy meadow and the wind moving the leaves of the tall trees that grew in the small wood that was close by. I had thrown down my heavy bike by the gate to the field and after walking up the steep incline to my favourite spot, I was still out of breath. It was an isolated place; that's why Dad didn't like me coming here on my own, but as I was meeting Jay later, I would only be alone for a little while. Dad probably wouldn't mind.

I took out my phone from my jeans pocket and squinted into the sunlight, trying to see what time it was or whether he had texted. We had agreed to meet at 11 and it was past that now. I was fuming. Why was Jay always late? Probably distracted by his new Wii U, or just forgotten what the time was. I let my fingers dip into the icy cold water of the stream. Jay would be in hot water when he finally got here!

Putting my phone back into my pocket I lay down again. I closed my eyes feeling drowsy. I may have drifted off to sleep for a moment or two. Then a scratchy sort of clanking noise made me sit up and rub my eyes sleepily. What was that noise? Was it Jay? I jumped onto my feet and stood on tip toe looking towards the place I thought the sound was coming from. There it was again! Curious, I started to make my way back to the gate, when suddenly, I saw a boy holding a bike. I smiled uncertainly and started to say hello when I realised, he had MY bike. He looked at me with a smirk shaping his thin lips, jumped on the bike and cycled off. I yelled at him to stop and quickly tried to climb over the gate to chase after him, but it was no good. By the time I had got to the other side he was just too far away and worst still was waving happily at Jay who waved back as he cycled towards me. I was going to be in so much trouble!

1. Why was the author out of breath?

A: Because his bike was heavy.

B: Because of the sun.

C: Because he had walked up a hill.

D Because it was a long way to the country

2. Why was the author's Dad worried about him coming to this particular place?

A: He was worried about his son getting lost.

B: He didn't want his son taking his bike into the field.

C: He was concerned about his son being alone in a place that was so quiet and hidden away.

D: He thought the bike was too heavy to ride that far.

3. Why did the author go back to the gate?

Option 1: Because he heard a strange noise.

Option 2: Because he thought Jay might have arrived.

Option 3: Because he thought he had left the gate open.

Option 4: Because he saw a boy.

A: Option 1 and 4

B: Option 1 and 2

C: Option 3 and 4

D: All of the options.

4. What does the phrase "Jay would be in hot water when he finally got here" mean?

A: The author thought that Jay would be so late, the hot sun would heat up the stream by the time he arrived.

B: The author was going to tell Jay off for being so late.

C: The author thought that Jay would be very hot when he arrived.

D: The author thought that Jay would want to paddle in the stream.

5. Why did the author go to the field even though he knew his Dad didn't want him to?

A: Because he was going to meet Jay and wouldn't be on his own for very long.

B: Because he was thirsty.

C: Because he thought his Dad was being silly.

D: Because Jay was late.

6. As used in this passage, what does the word 'fuming' mean?

A: smoky   B: sweating

C: very cross   D: very sad.

7. Why did Jay wave at the other cyclist?

A: Because he wanted to show him which way to go.

B: Because he wanted to let him know he had the wrong bike.

C: Because he tried to distract him to get the bike back.

D: Because he thought he knew him.

8. Which of the following best describes how the author's mood changes through the passage?

A: He was enjoying the sunshine happily, but cross because Jay was late, and his bike was stolen.

B: He was anxiously waiting for Jay to arrive and angry and cross because he was late and didn't stop the thief.

C: He was enjoying the sunshine but concerned about getting into trouble with Dad and then angry with Jay for being late, not realising his bike had been stolen and then concerned what his Dad would say.

D: He was tired but enjoying watching the crowds whilst wondering why his friend was late, but then curious about the strange sound that woke him up.

Answers:

1) C

2) C

3) B

4) B

5) A

6) C

7) D

8) C

8

Elements of the Exam: Non-Verbal Reasoning

What is non-verbal reasoning?

New to many when beginning their 11+ journey, adults and children alike, non-verbal reasoning questions assess a person's ability to look carefully at shapes, lines and patterns, and then discover an answer through logical deduction. It is something that some people find relatively easy, and they can thoroughly enjoy working out the puzzles of non-verbal questions, whilst others struggle to 'see' what makes one answer better than another. A positive aspect of non-verbal questions in the 11+ is that this component is very difficult to drastically improve upon through intense tuition. Non-verbal tests are often considered a reliable indicator of natural ability. Why not just use non-verbal question then, to decide upon who would suit a grammar school education?

Whilst these questions have their advantages, children that are highly imaginative seem to often find them quite tricky - seeing things in the pictures that are irrelevant and distract from the answer. Meanwhile, whilst less easy to teach, it is important that your child has some experience with these question types before the exam. Their unfamiliarity can be off-putting at first, but strategies that can employed to answer various types of question, and practice can improve performance.

We cannot say which question types will be used in any specific CEM exam, and it is possible that new types may be introduced. However, past papers have shown some consistency, and at least some of the types below are likely to appear.

Matching

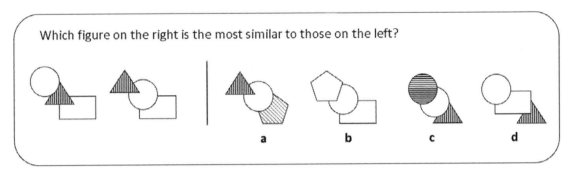

The answer is D, there are two white and one vertically striped shape.

Odd One Out

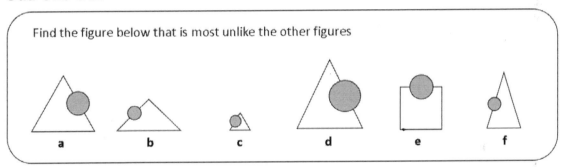

The answer is E, all the other main shapes are triangles.

Nets That Can Create a Shape

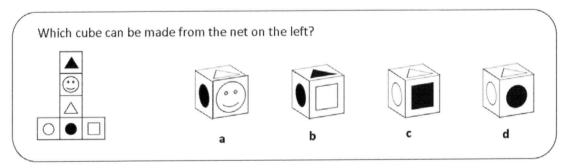

The answer is D, this is the only cube where the face positions match the net.

Shapes That Create a Net When Unfolded

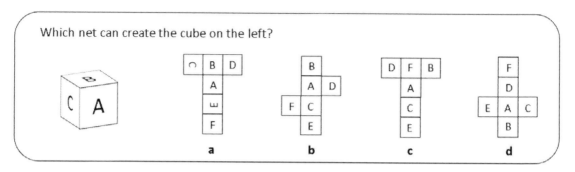

The answer is A, which is the only one where the appropriate sides match.

Reflections

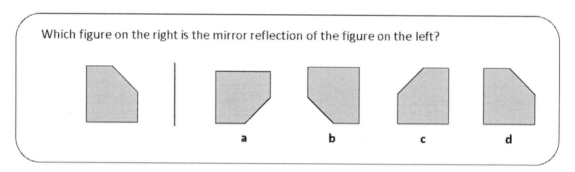

The answer is C, the others are not just a single reflection.

Hole Punching

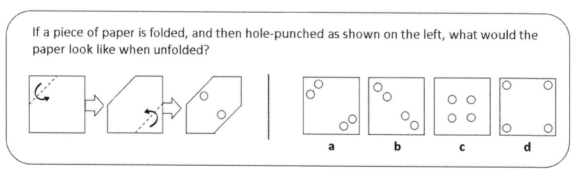

The answer is B, the other shapes do not have the holes correctly related.

Find a Figure to Complete a Series

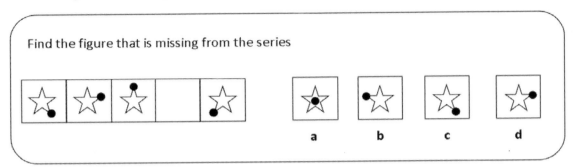

The answer is B, the black circle rotates anticlockwise around the star.

Vertical and Horizontal Codes

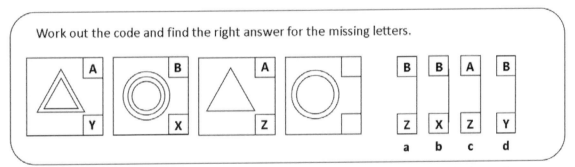

The answer is D – the letter B represents circles and Y represents two shapes.

Complete the Grid

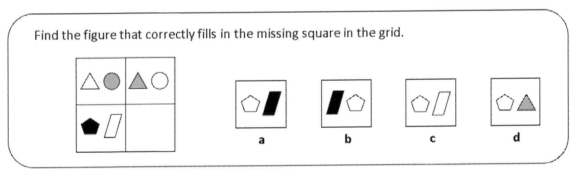

The answer is A, the bottom row has the correct shapes shaded appropriately.

Analogies - Complete the Pair

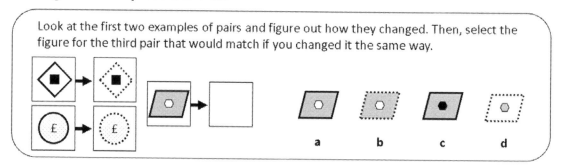

Look at the first two examples of pairs and figure out how they changed. Then, select the figure for the third pair that would match if you changed it the same way.

The answer is B, the outside line becomes dotted and the inside is unchanged.

Find the Bird's-Eye View for a Three-dimensional Shape

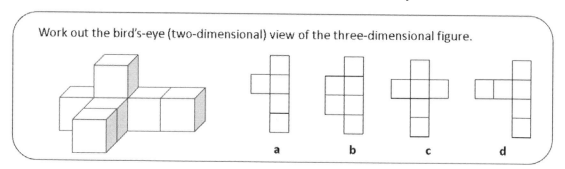

Work out the bird's-eye (two-dimensional) view of the three-dimensional figure.

The answer is D, it is the only plan view which matches.

Three Dimensional Rotations

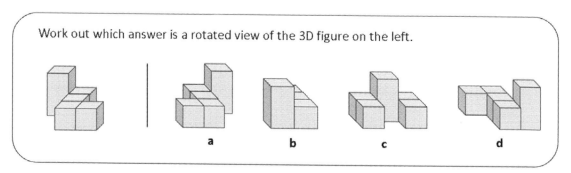

Work out which answer is a rotated view of the 3D figure on the left.

The answer is D, it is the view from the other end of the shape.

Block Building

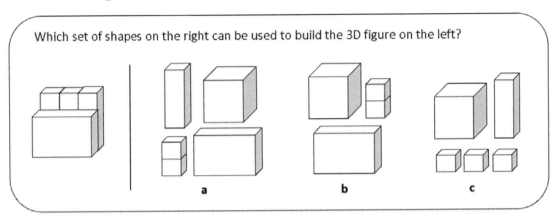

Which set of shapes on the right can be used to build the 3D figure on the left?

a   b   c

The answer is A, but note that some of the shape is hidden behind the blocks.

General tips for Non-Verbal Reasoning

- For most question types look for two possible answers. Find the difference between these two and compare them with the original shape.
- Look for the most obvious characteristics of images first to eliminate the most unlikely answers, but do not assume that finding these will be enough to find the complete answer - check for more than one characterising rule
- Lightly cross off answers that do not fit as you work

Considerations/Characteristics to Consider

Clockwise   - Are shapes arranged in a clockwise or anti-clockwise direction?

Colour   - How is it shaded?

Curves   - How are curves drawn? How many are there?

Size   - Do sizes vary?

Symmetry   - Is a shape symmetrical?

Shape   - What do certain shapes have in common?

Layering   - Shapes and lines may be layered in a variety of ways

Line type	- Lines may be dotted or dashed in different ways and vary in thickness
Length	- Length difference may vary but will not require perfect eyesight or measuring to see
Positioning	- Consider Direction and Position. Where do arrow point? Have shapes moved?
Angles	- Beware the size and number of angles a shape has
Number	- Counting is essential. If you can count in pairs all the better.
Turns	- Both two- and three-dimensional shapes may be rotated

It is best to learn and remember this or a similar mnemonic, and perhaps even write the letters on your scrap paper in the test.

<u>C</u>arol's <u>S</u>paniel <u>L</u>oves Pants - Remembering that there are three C, S and L words.

C	**S**	**L**	**P**	Positioning
Clockwise	Size	Layering	**A**	Angles
Colour	Symmetry	Line type	**N**	Number
Curves	Shape	Length	**T**	Turns
			S	Solved!

9

Elements of the Exam: Numerical Reasoning (Maths)

In the Gloucestershire 11+ exam you can expect to find two Maths sections, one primarily relating to short arithmetic questions, and the other asking for longer worded mathematical problems to be solved.

Short Numerical Reasoning

To be successful here your child must hone their mental arithmetic ability. Speed and accuracy are key. Improving estimating and number grouping skills is essential. Knowing when it is best to calculate mentally, and when to jot down a sum can make a huge difference and mental mathematical ability can improve dramatically playing lots of games with dice and playing cards. Unlike Year 6 SATS no marks will be given for workings shown so if your child can do calculations in their head and don't need to make notes, or at least just write down a few key numbers those extra few seconds really add up. It means they will have time to tackle the trickier questions and gain extra marks.

Below are some examples of quick ways to add and subtract. See if your child is already using these methods, and if not, encourage them to develop the habit of doing so.

Addition

Example 1	Example 2	Example 3
2351 + 401	3561 + 2932	5736 + 98
Does this even need to be written out? Does your child easily recognise that they can simply add to the hundreds and units' positions?	Can they cross the boundary between the thousands and hundreds to add these mentally?	Can they independently decide to add 100 and subtract 2?

Subtraction

Example 1	Example 2	Example 3
4975 - 3751	8379 - 99	6572 - 48
Does your child recognise that this requires no written method?	Subtract 100 and add one?	Subtract 50 and add two?

Be sure they are aware of the following:

odd + odd = even

even + even = even

odd + even = odd

If you are adding a list of numbers together the total will always be even unless there are an odd number of odd numbers

So, this list has a total which is odd: 37, 34, 29, 90, 66, 44, 37, 66, 15, 99

Multiplication and Division

Your child should know all their times tables, preferably to x12 without hesitation. If these are not yet learnt, we suggest it is their top priority before working on further maths questions for the 11+. However, there are numerous strategies to help your child out if they are stuck.

4 x 8 is the same as 4 x 4 x 2, or even 2 x 2 x 4 x 2

In the nine times table up to and including times ten, the digits of the answer add up to 9

$$1 \times 9 = 9 \qquad = 9$$

$$2 \times 9 = 18 \qquad 1 + 8 = 9$$

$$3 \times 9 = 27 \qquad 2 + 7 = 9$$

$$4 \times 9 = 36 \qquad 3 + 6 = 9$$

For more difficult questions, try **partitioning**

Multiplying by 12 can be done by partitioning by 10 and 2 and adding these.

$$12 \times 8 = 10 \times 8 = 80$$

$$2 \times 8 = 16$$

Answer: $80 + 16 = 96$

A little more difficult:

$$6 \times 24 = 6 \times 20 \text{ and } 6 \times 4 = 120 + 24 = 144$$

Even sums such as 34 x 23 can be accomplished quite easily mentally by some children; others may need to jot down just a few numbers to keep them on track.

34×23

$30 \times 20 = 600$ now add $30 \times 3 = 90$ so jot down 690

$4 \times 20 = 80$ now add $4 \times 3 = 12$ so jot down 92

Using mental addition add $690 + 92$ (do $690 + 100 = 790$ and subtract 8)

Answer: 782

If this is all getting a bit too complicated, be sure they remember that multiplying is just adding up the same number a certain number of times e.g. $15 \times 6 = 15 \times 15 \times 15 \times 15 \times 15 \times 15 = 90$!

How about multiplying by 99?

Multiply by 100 and then subtract the original number

$$37 \times 99 = (37 \times 100) - (1 \times 37) = 3700 - 37$$

How about $(56 \times 25) + (44 \times 25)$?

This is actually $100 \times 25 = 2500$ which is a lot easier!

When your child becomes confident manipulating numbers, far less is needed to be written and time spent on them. What is important is that they learn to look for as many short-cuts as possible without compromising accuracy.

If your child is proficient with multiplication, simple division should not cause too much difficulty. At this age some children will have moved on to long division, whilst others may still use clumping methods. Either are acceptable. In either case, remind them that multiple zeros can be added as necessary after a decimal point without altering the number (e.g. 4.05 = 4.050000). It is generally expected that the children can divide with decimals rather than putting remainders, although remainders may be useful for some questions.

Divisibility Rules

Knowing the following can come in handy.

- Any even number is divisible by 2
- Any number ending in 5 or 0 is divisible by 5 (Example: 945)
- Any number whereby the sum of the digits is divisible by 3, is also divisible by 3 (Example:321 or 504).
- If the last two digits are divisible by 4, the number is divisible by 4 (Example: 3032).
- If the number is even and divisible by 3, then it is divisible by 6 (Example 114).
- Double the last number and subtract it from the rest of the number. If that number is divisible by 7, the original number is too (Example: 672 2+2=4 67-4=63 63 is divisible by 7, so 672 must also be).
- If the last three digits are divisible by 8, the number is divisible by 8 (Example: 416).
- If the sum of the digits is divisible by 9, the number is divisible by 9 (Example 41,454).

Special Numbers

A working knowledge of these numbers is invaluable

Negative numbers

Most children are used to talking about negative numbers when discussing temperatures, and we find a vertical 'thermometer' diagram is often the easiest way to tackle negative number questions.

Things to remember:
- A large negative number is less than a small negative number
- Subtracting a minus is the same as adding a positive

Square number – any whole number multiplied by itself

Example: 5 x 5 = 25   8 x 8 = 64

Cube Number – any whole number multiplied by itself, and then again

Example: 5 x 5 x 5 = 125   3 x 3 x 3 = 27

Triangular Number – the number of dots in each triangular pattern. By enlarging a triangle by adding a new row, we are adding the next triangular number

Example: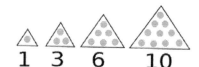

Factor – numbers which divide a whole number of times into another number

Example: Using a factor rainbow, the factors of 24 are

Multiple – a number that may be divided by another a certain number of times without a remainder

Example: 55 is a multiple of 11

Prime Number – a number which has no factors other than one and itself. (Note that 1 is NOT considered a prime number)

The first 10 prime numbers: 2, 3, 5, 7, 11, 13, 17, 19, 23, 29

Note: With the exception of number 2, there are no prime even numbers

Sequences

Number sequences are lists of numbers connected by patterns. The connections may include addition, subtraction, multiplication or division, or a combination of these.

Examples

1, 6, 11, 16 is a sequence increasing by 5 each time

2, 5, 9, 14, 20 is a sequence where the number increases by 3, 4, 5, 6 and so on

Hints for Sequence Questions

- Always check for square or cubed numbers first
- Be ready to use the four operations (add, subtract, multiply or divide) one or more times
- Work with the line from right to left if this is easier
- Seeing a 'skip' pattern that leap frogs in a regular pattern can help
- Write above or below the numbers anything that helps

Example:

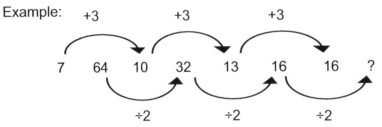

The answer is 8, 16 divided by 2.

- If the answer is not apparent, perhaps you need to check for triangular or prime numbers

- Short sequences are not necessarily easier

- Be prepared for negative numbers

The Fibonacci Sequence

This famous sequence, often found in nature, can appear on 11+ papers. In it, a set of numbers, proceeds based on the rule that the next number is the sum of the two preceding numbers.

Example:

0 1 1 2 3 5 8 13 21

Decimals, Fractions and Percentages

Decimals (Key points to remember)

- For adding or subtracting with decimals, remind your child of the importance of place value – lining up the decimal point and numbers in their correct value position before beginning.
- Multiplying with decimals is most easily achieved by removing the decimal point, doing the multiplication, and then 're-inserting into the correct position once the multiplication is complete. It helps if your child understands the reasoning behind this, rather than just applying the rule mechanically.
- When dividing with decimals, **do not** remove the decimal place; instead, line it up with the original number you are dividing.

Fractions

- **Adding and Subtracting Fractions**. The child that understands that different quantities of a whole cannot be added/subtracted effectively without being the same size, will understand that a common denominator must be used. It is best to demonstrate this with pictorial examples such as fractions of pizzas (with the whole pizza being the same size, but slices being different sizes).
- **Multiplying Fractions**. When dealing with fractions the terms multiply and 'of' are interchangeable. To explain what we mean when we are multiplying fractions, I draw a knitted scarf that has equal length sections.
  Example: A scarf divided into 12 equal length sections can be divided visually into quarters (three sections each), thirds (four sections each) and so on.
- **The Division of Fractions**. It is unlikely that these questions will occur in the 11+ test although rather annoyingly, they quite often occur in practice tests. As adults, many of us remember the rule 'turn the second fraction upside down and multiply across (take the reciprocal of the divisor and multiply the denominator), and using this rule, we can quickly achieve an answer to $\frac{3}{8}$ divided by 2/7. However, the multiple concepts involved in understanding the reasoning behind this rule are not usually expected to be understood by even very bright ten-year olds.

Your child should be aware that they may be asked about fractions in different ways.

Examples:

i. How many fifths are there in 11? (55)

ii. Mike is painting a fence. He has 18 posts. He paints ⅓ of them red. How many posts are not painted red? (12)

The importance of a thorough knowledge of multiplication facts and factors comes into play very soon.

Example:

A tin contains 24 biscuits and is shared out between 5 people. How many biscuits does each person get if they receive the fractions of the total below?

    Dan gets ⅙ (4)   George gets ⅛ (3)   Molly gets 1/12 (2)

    Alli gets ¼ (6)   Maya gets ⅜ (9)

Percentages

These are most easily explained by showing how the word percent is actually telling us that a number is a fraction out of 100.

$$15\% \text{ is the same as } 15/100$$

Fractions of a whole number can be done quickly by simple division

$$\tfrac{1}{5} \text{ of } 30 = \tfrac{1}{5} \times 30/1 = 30/5 = 6$$

When asked to find a percentage of a given amount it is often easiest for children to find 10% of a number and work from there.

$$10\% \text{ of } 40 = 4$$

$$\text{Therefore } 30\% \text{ of } 40 = 12$$

For more difficult calculations they could still use this method A, or the more advanced method, method B, described below.

Method A

43% of 960

10% = 96

40% = 96 x 4 = 384

1% = 9.6

3% = 28.8

384 + 28.8 = 412.8

Method B

43% of 960

43/100 x 960

0.43 x 960 = 412.8

Essential fractions/ percentage/decimal equivalents your child should know for the test:

$$25\% = 1/4 = 0.25$$

$$50\% = 1/2 = 0.5$$

$$75\% = 3/4 = 0.75$$

$$20\% = 1/5 = 0.2$$

$$12.5\% = 1/8 = 0.125$$

$$100\% = 1$$

Knowing these essential numbers, your child, faced with finding 12.5% of 56, can quickly divide 56 by 8.

Children may also be asked to turn a fraction into an unknown percentage or decimal.

To change any fraction into a percentage just multiply by 100 or move the decimal point two places to the right.

⅜ = 3 divided by 8 = 0.375 as a decimal or 37.5%. If your child finds this division quite difficult, their knowledge of ⅛ = 0.125 can help by adding it three times.

Example: 12.5 + 12.5 + 12.5 = 37.5%

Many of the problems involving the concepts above may also involve rounding. Your child should be aware of the convention of rounding 'up' if the next digit, the number directly after the place value of rounding expected is 5 or above, and down, if it is anywhere from 0 - 4.

Example: 400,357 rounded to the nearest hundred = 400,400

                    314,279 rounded to the nearest ten thousand = 310,000

Ratio and Proportion

It is relatively simple to explain the term proportion. It is a comparison of two numbers, each presenting part of a whole.

Example: In a bath of twelve white and brown eggs, there are 5 brown eggs. What proportion are white?

        There must be 7 white eggs and therefore the proportion is 7/12

Understanding ratio often poses more difficulty due to confusion with conventional fractions questions. Ratio is the balance between parts of a whole. Therefore, your child should first add up the figures to discover a total 'whole' in one situation, and then recognise the share of the component parts. Once this is clear, encourage them to imagine another 'whole' that is absolutely identical to the first, except for the size of the whole.

Example: A car park is full of red and green cars. All the spaces are full, with a capacity of 108 cars.

        If there are 24 red cars, there must be 84 green cars.

        This can be written as 24:84

What if there were another car park is twice the size? We would need to double the number of red cars and the number of green cars for them to make the same proportion of the whole.

This can be written as 48:168 with a total of 216 cars

Imagine if the car park was ½ the size of the original car park. We would need one third of the number of both red and green cars. The original park had 24 red cars and 84 green cars.

One-half can be written as 12:42 with a total of 54 cars.

The lowest ratio that could be found by finding the highest common factor of both 24 and 84, 12. Giving us the answer 2: 7, which would provide a car park for 9 cars.

Inversely, sometimes the children may be given a ratio in order to find a whole.

Example: While walking to work, John found that 2 in every 9 cars that drove past him were blue. Eight blues cars drove past him. What was the total number of cars that drove past John?

> 2:7 = a total of 9 cars. If there are 8 blue cars, that is four times larger than the original figure given, so there must be four times the seven given.
>
> Our new ratio is 8:28. Added together we have a total of 36 cars

Time

A wide variety of questions about the topic of time may come up during the 11+ exams. It is important to be competent using analogue clocks, digital time, as well as the twenty-four-hour clock.

A surprising number of children are not confident naming the months of the year, and the number of days in each month. To find the days of each month, it is best to use one of two strategies.

The Knuckle Method

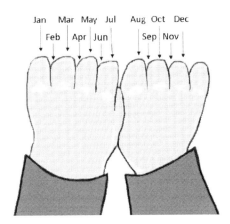

The Old Months' Rhyme

30 Days Have September

April, June and November

All the Rest Have 31

Except for February Alone

Which has but 28 Days Clear

And 29 in Each Leap Year

Time Tables

In our digital world, children are less experienced reading tables such as bus and time tables than in the past. Allow your child to work out times using these in a practical way whenever possible.

When working out time calculations it is often useful for children to use a timeline. Some children will be tempted to try to add or subtract times using column addition, but of course, as our time is not measured in base ten, this is not a suitable method. Others may easily add/subtract hours then minutes mentally and by jotting down a few figures work out the correct answer.

When adding time, the phrases 'Using time, cross the line' can help.

Example: 3 hrs 54 mins + 2 hrs 36 mins can be written as below with the vertical line dividing the hours and the minutes.

3	54
2	36
6	30

Two Dimensional Shapes and Angles

Ensure your child remembers these basics, creating flash cards if necessary:

- Can you name all regular two-dimensional shapes with up to ten sides?
- The perimeter of a shape is the outside edge, I often describe as the 'fence'. This is a long word, which might help your child to make a connection - that it matches all the way around a shape - the 'long' way. Many children slip up by confusing the terms area and perimeter
- The area of a square or rectangle is base x height
- The area of a triangle discovered either by base x height divided by two (as all triangles are made of two quadrilaterals), or put another way, ½ base x height
- The area of a parallelogram is base x height (even if lengths of other sides are given, just to throw them off!)
- Angles of a triangle add up to 180 degrees
- Angles of a quadrilateral add up to 360 degrees (again, two angles make one quadrilateral)
- Name four types of angle - right angle, acute, obtuse, reflex
- Recognise and name the properties of scalene, right angled, isosceles, equilateral
- Recognise and name parts of a circle - radius, diameter, circumference. (It may again help to remember that as circumference is a long word for 'all the way around', the radius is the shortest word and the shortest distance, and diameter between the two in both word length and as part of the circle)
- Angles between two consecutive numbers on a clock are 30degrees
- The angle sizes on a compass i.e. South and East = 90 degrees, between North and South East = 135 degrees
- Alternate angles, 'Z' angles are equal
  Example:

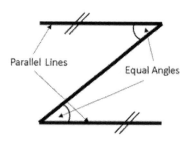

Parallel Lines

Equal Angles

- Opposite angles, 'X' angles are equal
  Example:

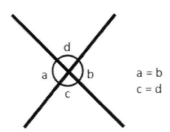

$a = b$
$c = d$

It is useful for your child to understand how each time a new side is added to a straight sided shape; the sum of the angles increases by 180 degrees. This can make sense to them by showing that by adding a side you are creating a new triangle.

It may be that the child is expected to work out a perimeter or area of an irregular shape based on information given. In such case, lengths may need to be deduced from what is in front of them. Often it is best to break the shape into manageable sections.

Example:

Find the perimeter of the irregular shape below:

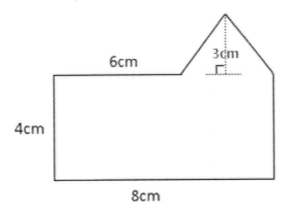

Answer:
Rectangle perimeter = 8 + 8 + 4 + 4 = 24
Triangle perimeter = 3 + 1 + (3^2 + 1^2) = 14
Total = 24 + 14 = 38

Bearings

Another topic, possibly new to your child, is being asked to find the bearing. Bearings measure direction or angle of movement. Three important facts about bearings:

- Bearings are **always measured from the north in degrees**.

- Bearings are only measured in a **clockwise** direction.

- Bearings are always shown with three digits. Even if the angle is just 23 degrees, it is written as 023

Encourage your child to beware of the language in these questions, how a bearing from B to A differs from A to B as this can be very confusing.

Example:

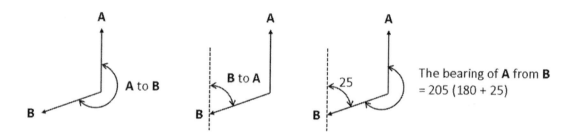

Coordinates, Transformations, and Rotation About a Point

Being able to deal with shapes and points and confidence in co-ordinates is a valuable skill to develop for the 11+ test. Some children find these more challenging than others but some extra work to improve these skills will be time well spent.

Coordinates

Most children appear to enjoy working out co-ordinates. A fun activity to secure how to work them out is the games of battleships. It helps to remember the mantra:

'**Along the corridor, then up the stairs**' in order to look at the x (horizontal) before the y (vertical) axis.

They should be comfortable using both grids with both positive and negative numbers.

Example:

What shape do you find when plotting these coordinates? (-4,2) (-2,3) (1,1) (1, -2)

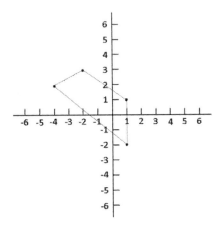

Answer: A Trapezium

Transformations

These are a little trickier, requiring the child to move an image by following directions

Example: Move the rectangle 3 squares north and two squares east.

In this case, it is easiest to move one point at a time, rather than 'lift' the entire shape. Think of sliding it along.

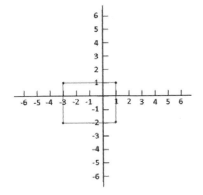

80

Rotation about a point

This shape is rotated 180° with the centre of rotation at coordinate (4,3)

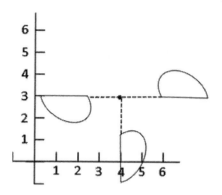

Three Dimensional Shapes

Know these key words and their meaning:

- Vertex (plural – vertices): is a corner
- Face: a single flat surface
- Edge: is a line segment between faces
- Depth: is the distance from the top to the bottom or front to back of the shape (the 'third' dimension)

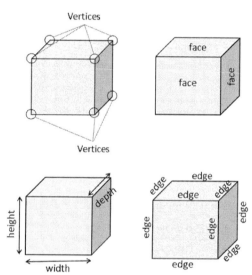

Volume

Some children will be unfamiliar with finding the volumes of shapes and are often unsure of what volume really means.

The volume of a shape is the space an object fills. With a loaf of bread, it would be the amount of bread that fills the loaf shape.

Ideally you would have plastic interlinking cubes on hand, with which to practically demonstrate volume, but aligned more conveniently to everyday lives at home, a loaf of bread will suffice. Your child will already be familiar with finding areas of rectangles, and is likely to understand that the area of a single slice of bread would be its width x height. Looking now at the 'depth' of the slice, we can suggest that it doesn't go back far – let's call its depth '1' (luckily it is usually close to one centimetre). When we want to find the volume of this slice of bread, we need to know the area of this one slice e.g. width 7cm x height 9cm = 63 cm squared, multiply by one to find the volume = 63 cubed. Perhaps they can imagine cutting it into these small cubes - you could even try! To find the volume of a whole loaf - that is all the bread that fills and creates the loaf, we need to see how many slices there are, say 25. Therefore, our volume is 63 (height x width) x 25 = 1,575 cm cubed. Once your child is comfortable with this, finding volumes for other regular shapes can come into play such as that of a triangular prism (base x height divided by two) area of one triangular end x depth. Now, these can be interchanged. E.g. If the volume and area of one end a cuboid is 12, and the volume is 96, the length must be 8. Even some irregular shape volumes can be worked out, if the depth is consistent.

Example:

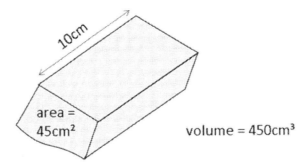

volume = 450cm³

Nets

Nets of three-dimensional shapes are components of both maths and Non-Verbal Reasoning sections in the 11+. We have discussed them in detail in the non-verbal reasoning section in Chapter 8.

Symmetry

Two types of symmetry are mentioned during 11+ preparation, regular mirror symmetry such as your child learnt about when painting butterflies in the infants, though now they must remember that the line of symmetry may be horizontal, vertical or diagonal. This is relatively simple, although some children struggle when needing to count distance from a mirror line. If this is the case, give them lots of practice using squared paper.

Example: If the top left shape is reflected in the diagonal line which shape is produced? (The answer is B)

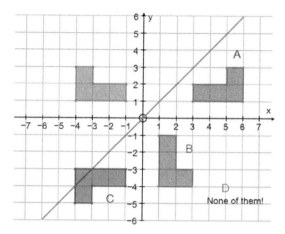

In all my years of tutoring I have yet to come across a child that could easily answer, this quite regular 11+ question:

How many lines of symmetry (regular) does a parallelogram have?

Many a child has attempted to prove the point that it has at least one line as we have cut out the shape to see. Occasionally children have taken the said cut-out shape home, determined to bring it back the following week to prove their point!

The second type of symmetry is called *rotational symmetry*. A shape's degree of rotational symmetry is the number of times it looks exactly the same following distinct turns. I find the best way to explain this is to remind the children of the wooden shape toy toddler's often have (perhaps they had one themselves), and then asking them to consider the number of different ways a shape could fit into the space given. This is the order of rotational symmetry that a shape has.

Example: What is the order of rotational symmetry for this shape?   Answer: 6 (Hexagon)

A kite would have just one, an equilateral triangle, three, a rectangle two. An interesting one is a circle - this would be an infinite number.

Probability

Probability can range from quite simple questions regarding likelihood, to complex questions which require the consideration of previous events in order to predict a likely future event

   a. The chances of your birthday being on a day beginning with T are 2 in 7

   b. The chances on scoring a four on a regular dice are 1/6

   c. The probability of scoring a total of twelve using two dice is 1/36

   d. From a bag of 6 red and 5 blue marbles, the probability of picking a red after a first blue marble is 6/10 = 3/5

Regularly playing games with dice and playing cards is very worthwhile.

Algebra

The term is quite scary to many, perhaps because we imagine white boards covered with a strange mathematical language beyond our comprehension, but with the children I like to introduce the topic by letting them know that without knowing it they have been working towards this for many years already. I remind them of the 'missing number sums' they encountered in the infants such as 6 +? = 10 and explain that this is what algebra is all about – using letters or symbols in place of numbers to represent values where the exact value is not yet known. It doesn't seem quite so daunting then. I explain that 'x' is commonly used for the unknown quantity, but that it could be any symbol or letter. A new point that does need to be addressed is that in algebra the multiplication sign between the number of a quantity and the symbol for the quantity is removed.

Example: 3 x B (perhaps meaning B for beetles) would be written as 3B. This takes a bit of getting used to for most learners.

Sample Question   a. 3y = 21. What is the value of y? Answer: 7

                     b. 2k + 6 = 26. What is the value of k? Answer: 10

Algebra is also applied to longer worded maths questions:

Let's imagine that we want to find the number of legs on a number of spiders. Presuming each spider had eight legs, we would multiply the number of spiders by 8. If we give the number of spiders as x, the number of legs will be 8x. We could work out the number of legs on any number of spiders now.

Once this way of expressing unknown numbers is understood, we can work out correct expressions represent a worded problem

Sarah wishes to go to the cinema with her 3 friends and share a bag of popcorn costing £4. The tickets cost an amount y. Which expression below shows the total cost of this trip for the friends together in pounds.

A	B	C	D	E
3y4	4y +4	4y + 3	3y +4y	y – 4

The answer is B 4y+4. There is a total of four people so the tickets cost 4y. In addition, they spend 4 pounds on one bag of popcorn.

Estimation

Really hard maths questions can be a lot easier with multiple choice, which you can expect to find in at least one of the maths sections in the test. Using powers of estimation, the tricky question below is simple. Twelve times five is sixty, and only one of these answers comes relatively close to that.

Question   12.6 x 5.5

Options	A	B	C	D	E
	0.0693	6.93	693	0.693	69.3

Data Questions

These may include charts including tally/frequency charts, pie charts, line and bar graphs, pictograms and other ways of displaying information. Many of these display data in a way in which is quite familiar, but it is the 'devil in the details' and misleading data that are problematic.

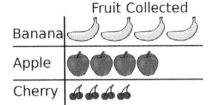

Examples: Misleading picture size

Venn diagram – name/number in the box but not in a group

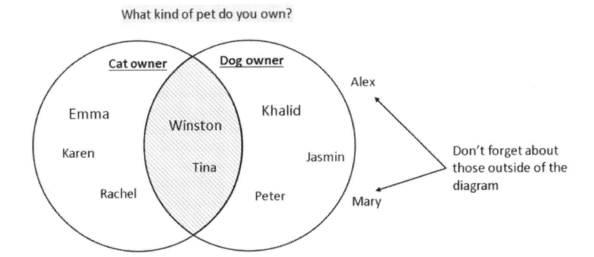

Worded Problems

All of the above strategies and levels of knowledge are also essential for achieving high marks with worded mathematical reasoning questions. Even children that usually love Maths can come unstuck here.

The key is to recognise each component part of the question before attempting to answer it. Then, when the main calculations are complete, they must see if they have missed anything, particularly a final part? Whereas we suggest that under-lining key features may not help with comprehension questions, it can be a lot more useful here. A suggestion that works well for some children is that they write the mathematical sign connected to each component apart above the words, before starting the whole. Whichever strategy you choose to use, your child should be aware of three key points.

1. The order that the questions are presented in will not reflect the difficulty of the task and therefore it may be worth picking out easier questions to do sooner

2. If the figures being used are becoming increasingly difficult to manage such as 3.777 recurring, it is likely that a mistake has been made earlier in the calculations. If this is the case it is best to see if it is easy to correct, or circle the question number, leave the question for now, and given enough time, return to later.

3. Utilising the answer choices for multiple choice questions provides an advantage using logical estimation and deduction.

Experience suggests that this is a very speed intensive section, and it is not unusual for many children not to complete it. This does not necessarily mean that this will not gain a place at a grammar school.

10

Mock Tests

How to Prepare

Whether you have a tutor or are helping your child yourself, one of the questions we hear most often is 'How can I help them revise and prepare for the test?'. There's clearly no single answer to this question but it is worth looking at the value of mock tests and other revision and preparation techniques.

Mock Tests

A few years ago, there were few opportunities for children to have a realistic practice of the 11+ test, but today there are a range of national and local providers offering Mock Tests with reports on your child's performance. But are they worth doing?

The short answer is yes, because if nothing else, your child will be able to go through the whole process of what will happen on the real day. They will probably be very nervous going to the Mock, but they will probably be less stressed on the real test day, because they have already gone through the process. It's possible that the Mock Test isn't administered in exactly the same way as the real test, but it will be similar enough to increase confidence in approaching the test day.

When Should My Child Start Taking Mock Tests?

If your child is going to try some mock tests it needs to be taken early enough for there to be sufficient time to act on any recommendations from the test. This means there should be at least a few weeks before the real test which takes place in the middle of September.

It's also advisable not to start the tests too soon to avoid 'test fatigue', although this will vary with each child, since some love doing as many tests as possible.

In any case, it is usually best to break up tests into smaller parts at the beginning to work up to longer tests later in Year 5. Most Mock Tests are held from around March onwards right through to the start of September.

How Many Mock Tests Should My Child Take?

This is another difficult question with no definitive answer and depends very much on your child. We would recommend that your child attends at least one independently administered test where there are other children present and the test is run under examination conditions. Many children will sit a couple of mock tests but doing more than this may not necessarily be especially valuable in terms of getting your child used to test conditions. Some parents find it useful to chart their child's progress through mock test reports but avoid putting your child through 'burn out' where they become thoroughly sick of the process and may not take the 'real' test seriously.

How to Choose the Right Mock Test

It's safe to say that most mock tests will be helpful in terms of getting your child used to being in examination conditions with other children under timed conditions. It will help them get used to the nervousness we all feel when we take a test and they won't be able to ask for help with the questions.

However, to get the most out of an 11+ mock test, it's important to look for certain features of the test:

- The test must be of the 'CEM' style covering comprehension, verbal reasoning, non-verbal reasoning and numerical reasoning (maths).
- The test must be set as two papers of around 45 minutes with a refreshment break in between
- The papers must have discrete sections which are timed individually and announced by the invigilators. Children should not be allowed to go back and amend their answers from previous sections
- Answers should be marked on a separate answer sheet, provided to the students. This should be marked in pencil to allow corrections.

- Questions should all be multiple choice, apart from some maths questions which should be free choice, where the answer is marked on the sheet using a small box for each digit.
- The invigilators should be friendly, supportive, knowledgeable and DBS cleared
- A detailed report should be provided covering the following information as a minimum:
  - Your child's overall score/percentage
  - An overall rank of your child in comparison to other students taking the test
  - A breakdown of score and ranking for each question type (comprehension, verbal, non-verbal and numerical reasoning):

The following are also highly desirable in the report:

- An invigilators' observation report, outlining how your child seemed to react to the test conditions - e.g. did they seem upset, could they sit quietly and calmly, were they distracted by others in the room
- A comparison with students taking the same test in previous years. Did students with similar scores obtain a place in grammar school and if so, which one?
- Recommendations provided to help improve performance on the test
- A local company with experience of the CEM test and local grammar schools
- Parents will often want to get the question papers and answer sheets to go through with their child to see what they got wrong. This seems to be a reasonable expectation but there are other things that need to be taken into account.

Should I Expect to See the Mock Question Paper?

If you do get the question papers and answer sheets for your mock test you will be able to go through the questions that they got wrong. However, bear in mind they will not be getting these questions in the real test and it won't really help too much for the real test. If the mock test providers keep back the question paper it has the advantage of reusing the paper in future years. The means scores from previous years can be compared with results from this year. By discovering which school children from previous years were allocated it is possible to predict which grammar schools (if any) are a realistic option for children taking the test this year.

Should I Show the Report to my Child?

This is something you must decide for yourself. You know your child better than anyone else and can share appropriate information from the mock report. You may wish to give them an overall idea of their result, rather than the exact ranking, to give a positive slant on their performance. However, it is important to be honest and realistic with your child to help them manage their expectations. For example, the rank may be particularly good for some question types, but rather low for others. This means they can focus on areas for more practice.

The report may suggest your child had a low ranking and is unlikely to secure a grammar school place. In this event you may decide not to go ahead with the 11+ test, or you may wish to focus on particular areas and have a second test to gauge any improvement.
No matter what the outcome of the mock test you should use this information together with other evidence you have of your child's ability to give a rounded view. In particular one bad mock test result among a lot of positive indications should not put you off as your child may just have had an 'off day' or the particular questions were unfamiliar to them. Try to determine if the result is atypical and consider if an additional mock test might be helpful.

11

Preparing for the Test Day

You may have spent many months preparing your child (and yourself!) for the 11+ test, but it's also good to prepare for the whole test day from the time you wake up to the time they walk out of the test school. Even then the day is not over as you may need to deal with their reaction to the test. Being prepared for the day means you can minimise the stress and make it as positive as possible.

Tiredness may be a fear your child has, particularly as the worry of taking the test might make them find it difficult to sleep the night before. If you make sure your child has good nights' sleep over the week before the test, and they struggle to sleep the night before, you can assure them that they are reasonably well rested. They are likely to be reasonably alert in the morning and fatigue may not catch up with them until after the test.

Exam Technique for your Child

It's useful to have a quick refresher just before the test to remember the basics of how to maximise your marks by using a few simple techniques.

- Leave no answer blank on multiple choice questions. Firstly, try to eliminate wrong answers, and then pick from those you believe most likely. If you feel you haven't got a clue, pick one letter (lots of people choose 'C') and use it consistently for unknown questions.
- Circle all the answers you are unsure of or have guessed completely. You may have the opportunity to revisit them when you have completed others. You can put a line through this circle if you suspect that amongst other circled questions, you believe it to be especially difficult, and least likely to be successfully worked out.
- Keep working until the last second.
- Be certain to only give one answer for each question unless otherwise stated, and to mark the answer sheet exactly as required.

- For any corrections rub out previous answers completely and then fill in the new one. Remember that a computer will mark this exam and will mark anything wrong that it detects with multiple answers for one question where there should be just one.
- Be realistic regarding which sums/spellings to do mentally and which need a pencil a paper.
- If your last five answers have been 'A', and you believe your next answer is also 'A', do not be influenced by your previous answers. Go ahead and put A; do not change the others either.
- Use your finger to check the place that you are writing an answer and be sure not to accidentally miss an answer box.
- Do not spend long on any question. Short easy questions score just as many points as more difficult ones.
- Use the scrap paper provided effectively.

We do not recommend that you use a watch for this exam, and in fact, watches are likely to be disallowed as a digital watch may be used to as tool for some questions. Although there is a clock in the room, we suggest that you ignore it for judging how much time is available. The reason for this is that each section will be individually timed with notice of time left given in parts. If you rely on a clock/watch, you may be distracted

looking at it rather than simply working as quickly as you can – it is not easy to follow the time on a test like this anyway.

It is not unlikely that there will be some disturbance during your exam. Perhaps someone can't stop coughing, scrape their chair regularly, may whisper, or are sick. We have even heard rumours of someone snoring! Whoever is making this noise could be your friend. You must try to ignore all distractions and set aside your feelings. If the distraction is too much, the adult (invigilator), will probably notice it too and make arrangements, if not, you may raise your hand and tell them. For any less serious distraction, where you can keep working but it is an annoyance, you may mention it to this adult at the end of the section or test (whichever is appropriate).

Always remind yourself that you are competing against other candidates, not against the test paper. However easy or difficult you find it, others will find it easy or difficult too. Just do the best that you can do.

Test Day Advice for Children

- You are likely to be nervous, and although this doesn't feel nice, it is just your body preparing you to be ready; and is likely to subside once the testing starts.
- Eat a sensible breakfast, not substantially different from what you would normally have
- Wear layers of clothes in order to be prepared whatever the temperature in the test room.
- Never Give Up! This test is designed to be difficult. It is a chance for you to show what you can do.

Make sure to:

- Go to the loo before the exam and during the break. You will not be given extra time at the end of the test to complete parts missed because you had to go!
- Use all of the exam techniques that you have learnt.
- During the break, do not be influenced by what others might say about what they thought of Paper 1
- Know that this is just one of many opportunities that you will have in life, and that acceptance or not into a grammar school is not an indication of how successful you will be in life.

Test Day Advice for Parents!

- Ensure that you bring all the necessary paper work for the exam. The exact requirements will be stipulated closer to the test but are likely to include a candidate number and colour (you will have been sent these) and photo ID.
- Pack a snack with a drink that is not too large
- Perhaps suggest a banana on the journey to the test centre
- Check the route to the centre and parking before hand
- Arrive in plenty of time
- Discourage your child from bringing a mascot or charm - imagine if it went missing!

Reassure your child and offer them a show of confidence. Let your child know how proud you are of them; they have already achieved, and all their hard work will give them a great start to Year 6!

After the exam show your appreciation of the fact that your child will have worked extremely hard all morning. They are likely to be quite tired, but most will appreciate doing something that they really enjoy in the afternoon.

Try not to bombard your child with questions are the test. What is done is done. The only question that could be of consequence now, is whether there were any disturbances or other reason that they may not have been able to perform to the best of their ability. If anything has arisen, now would be the time to mention it to the school.

12

Appeals

What are Appeals?

An appeal is a way of gaining a place at your preferred school by indicating that this is a more suitable or appropriate school than the one you have been allocated. You would generally only appeal if you are dissatisfied with the school that you have been allocated by the County Council.

The appeals process is structured in a particular way and it is important you follow the due process for appealing against your school allocation in order for it to have any chance of succeeding. It is not enough to say you are not happy with the school you have been given, there has to be a stronger argument to support your case.

The appeals process works in the same way for all Gloucestershire school places the same, regardless of whether you are applying for grammar or comprehensive school.

Why Would I Appeal?

You would usually only appeal if you are not satisfied with the school that you have ended up with on reallocation at the end of March. You do not need to start appeal proceedings until this point, as outlined in earlier chapters of this book. However, you may suspect that an appeal is going to be likely, if the school you were allocated at the beginning of March was not one you are satisfied with. In this case it might be worth putting together evidence for your case, in advance, to save extra work later.

When Can I Appeal?

You would usually appeal after Allocation Day at the beginning of March. All grammar schools in Gloucestershire are independent academies and you must send appeals directly to them. The window where you must send an appeals form is usually from the start to the end of April and appeals will be heard in May or June.

How Do I Appeal?

Once you have downloaded the appeals form for each of the schools that you wish to appeal for, you will need to complete them and send them back to each of the schools by the deadline.

You generally have a week or two after this deadline to submit any additional paperwork to support your appeal. This may be a letter from your headteacher, a note from a doctor or other health professional stating that your child was not well on the day of the test or the time leading up to the test, SATS results or a Mock Test report comparing their performance with others taking the test. It is important to focus this information and evidence so that it addresses the grounds of your appeal and is clearly relevant.

You can find the relevant forms, deadlines and further details on the appeals process on each of the Gloucestershire grammar school websites.

What Are the Grounds of Appeal?

If you are appealing for your child to be granted admission to a particular school you must ensure you focus this appeal in accordance with the grounds that are accepted for an appeal.

Your appeal will not be successful if it is based on proximity to the school, travel arrangements, sibling links, potential contribution to school life (academically or sporting, dislike of other schools or potential upset or disappointment at not getting the school. Appeals will only be successful if they are based on either the allocation process not being correctly applied or that your child's performance on the 11+ test was significantly affected by some factor.

It is rare that the allocation process has not been properly followed and it may be very difficult to obtain evidence to demonstrate this. The most likely grounds for a successful appeal is that the performance in the 11+ test was not typical of what your child would normally expect to achieve. This can also be difficult to demonstrate, so it's crucial that you gather any evidence of sickness or family trauma as soon as possible after the test. Examples of instances which are most likely to lead to a successful appeal are death of a close family member, break up of a close family relationship (especially mother and father) or significant physical illness on the day. This is not to say that other factors would not be successful and there is a small element of subjectivity depending on the people on the appeals panel.

Should I Attend the Appeals Panel Hearing?

We would always recommend that you attend the Appeals Panel meeting yourself if at all possible as you will be able to talk to the panel and this can give more weight to your appeal. You are allowed to take an 'advocate' with you which can be a member of your family, a friend or a professional advisor. This can help the process seem a little less intimidating and they may be able to talk on your behalf if you get tongue tied and are not sure what to say.

What Happens in the Appeals Panel Hearing?

The appeals panel consists of three members. One is lay (no connection with education), one non-lay (that has knowledge of education) and the third can be lay or non-lay. There  will also be an independent Clerk that can advise the panel on legal aspects of the appeal. The school will have a Presenting Officer that will enter and leave the panel hearing with you.

After introductions the school and the parents each put their case and may be asked questions by the appeals panel. When this has been done, the school and then the parents sum up and the clerk will record the details.

After the Presenting Office and parent(s) have left the panel will make their decision. You will hear the outcome in writing within 5 days of the hearing.

What if My Appeal Isn't Successful?

If you are not successful with your appeal there is no right of appeal against this decision. The only recourse is if you believe the appeal hearing itself was not conducted properly.

If your child achieved the qualifying standard but have not been allocated a grammar school place, you may still secure a place if you are on the waiting list.

You may need to accept that a grammar school place is not going to be a realistic possibility, but there might still be a chance of obtaining a place in future school years. More details on the appeals process and in-year admissions are available at the grammar school websites.

Finally…

We hope you've found this book useful in preparing your child for grammar school entrance. You may find it helpful to return to different sections as you move through the different stages of application, learning and testing.

We recognise that grammar school is not right for everyone and many children thrive at comprehensive schools. We wish you all the best for your child and hope that this volume has encouraged you to see this time as an opportunity to spend positive time together. Learning is never a waste and your child will find their grammar school preparation useful for future studies wherever that is.

We'd love to hear your stories and comments on whether you found this book useful. Please let us know if you have any suggestions on other things we should include in the book and we'll include them in future editions! In particular, it would really help us if you would write an Amazon review to help other potential readers decide if they should get a copy. We read every review as we love to know what you think.

If you'd like to find out more about our meetings and events, including mock tests, please go to our website www.cotswoldeducation.co.uk. If you have any questions or just want to have a chat about anything grammar school drop us an email and we'll get back to you.

Finally, please remember that whatever happens, it will end up being OK,

Liz and Ian

info@cotswoldeducation.co.uk

13

Resources

Books

We do not recommend that these books are bought all at once. We suggest that you pick one or two from verbal reasoning, maths and non-verbal reasoning initially, alongside some vocabulary materials, and buy more books over time. You may find resources that are equally useful, and where book one of a set has been indicated, we suggest you buy the next or something similar when completed.

English and Verbal Reasoning

Publisher: CGP

- New 11+ CEM Verbal Reasoning Practice Book & Assessment Tests - Ages 10-11 (with Online Edition) (CGP 11+ CEM)
- New 11+ CEM Verbal Reasoning Study Book (with Parents' Guide & Online Edition) (CGP 11+ CEM)
- New 11+ CEM 10-Minute Tests: Comprehension - Ages 10-11 Book 1 (with Online Edition) (CGP 11+ CEM)
- New 11+ CEM 10-Minute Tests: Verbal Reasoning Cloze - Ages 10-11 Book 1 (with Online Edition) (CGP 11+ CEM)
- New 11+ CEM 10-Minute Tests: Verbal Reasoning Vocabulary - Ages 10-11 (with Online Edition) (CGP 11+ CEM)
- New 11+ CEM 10-Minute Tests: Verbal Reasoning - Ages 10-11 Book 1 (with Online Edition) (CGP 11+ CEM)
- New 11+ CEM Verbal Reasoning Practice Question Cards - Ages 10-11 (CGP 11+ CEM)

Publisher: Eleven Plus Exams

- 11+ Essentials English Comprehensions: Classic Literature Book 1: First Past the Post
- 11+ Essentials English Comprehensions: Non-Fiction Book 1 (First Past the Post)
- 11+ Essentials English Mini Comprehensions: Inference Book 1 (First Past the Post)
- 11+ Essentials English Comprehensions: Contemporary Literature Book 1 (First Past the Post)
- 11+ Essentials Verbal Reasoning: Cloze Tests Book 1 (First Past the Post)
- 11+ Essentials Verbal Reasoning: Vocabulary in Context Level 4 (First Past the Post)
- 11+ Essentials Verbal Reasoning: Vocabulary Multiple Choice Practice Papers for CEM Book 2 (First Past the Post)
- 11+ Essentials Verbal Reasoning: Vocabulary Book 1: First Past the Post

Publisher: The Armadillo's Pillow Ltd

- The Big 11+ Vocabulary Play Book
- The 11+ Vocabulary Word Search Extravaganza
- The Survival Guide to Seriously Slippery Spellings

Publisher: Letts

- 11+ Vocabulary Flashcards (Letts 11+ Success)
- 11+ English and Verbal Reasoning Quick Practice Tests Age 10-11 for the CEM Assessment tests (Letts 11+ Success)
- 11+ Comprehension Results Booster for the CEM tests: Targeted Practice Workbook (Letts 11+ Success)

Publisher: Bond

- 11+ Essentials Verbal Reasoning: Vocabulary Book 1: First Past the Post
- Bond 11+: English and Verbal Reasoning Assessment Papers for the CEM 11+ tests: 10-11+ years
- Bond 11+: English & Verbal Reasoning CEM 10 Minute Tests: 10-11 years
- Bond 11+: CEM Vocabulary 10 Minute Tests: 10-11 Years

Recommended Reading List

The Wolves of Willoughby Chase, Joan Aiken

Artemis Fowl (series of eight novels), Eoin Colfer

The Dark is Rising, Susan Cooper

Walk Two Moons, Sharon Creech

Carrie's War, Nina Bawden

Skellig, David Almond

The Lost World, Arthur Conan Doyle

Lionboy, Zizou Corder

The Great Elephant Chase, Gillian Cross

The Village by the Sea, Anita Desai

An Angel for May, Melvin Burgess

Icefire, Chris d'Lacey

Holly Moon's Incredible Book of Hypnotism, Georgia Byng

The Kin, Peter Dickinson

Street Child, Berlie Doherty

Powder Monkey: The Adventures of Sam Witchall, Paul Dowswell

Maths

Publisher: CGP

- New 11+ CEM Maths Practice Book & Assessment Tests - Ages 10-11 (with Online Edition) (CGP 11+ CEM)
- New 11+ CEM Maths Study Book (with Parents' Guide & Online Edition) (CGP 11+ CEM)
- New 11+ CEM 10-Minute Tests: Maths - Ages 10-11 Book 1 (with Online Edition) (CGP 11+ CEM)
- New 11+ CEM 10-Minute Tests: Maths Word Problems - Ages 10-11 Book 1 (with Online Edition) (CGP 11+ CEM)

- New 11+ CEM Maths Practice Question Cards - Ages 10-11 (CGP 11+ CEM)
- New 11+ CEM 10-Minute Tests: Maths Quick Questions - Ages 10-11 (with Online Edition) (CGP 11+ CEM)

Publisher: Eleven Plus Exams

- 11+ Essentials Mathematics: Worded Problems Book 1 (First Past the Post)
- 11+ Essentials Mathematics: Mental Arithmetic Book 1 (First Past the Post)
- 11+ Essentials Numerical Reasoning: Multi-Part Book 1 (First Past the Post)
- 11+ Essentials Numerical Reasoning: Quick-Fire Book 1 - Multiple Choice (First Past the Post)
- 11+ Reference Mathematics Dictionary Plus (First Past the Post)

Publisher: Bond

- Bond 11+: Maths Assessment Papers: 10-11+ years Book

Non-Verbal Reasoning

Publisher: CGP

- New 11+ CEM Non-Verbal Reasoning Practice Book & Assessment Tests - Ages 10-11 (with Online Edition) (CGP 11+ CEM)
- New 11+ CEM Non-Verbal Reasoning Practice Question Cards - Ages 10-11 (CGP 11+ CEM)
- New 11+ CEM 10-Minute Tests: Non-Verbal Reasoning - Ages 10-11 Book 1 (with Online Edition) (CGP 11+ CEM)
- New 11+ CEM 10-Minute Tests: Non-Verbal Reasoning 3D & Spatial - Ages 10-11 Book 1 (with Online Ed) (CGP 11+ CEM)
- New 11+ CEM Non-Verbal Reasoning Practice Question Cards - Ages 10-11 (CGP 11+ CEM)
- New 11+ CEM 10-Minute Tests: Non-Verbal Reasoning 3D & Spatial - Ages 10-11 Book 1 (with Online Ed) (CGP 11+ CEM)

Publisher: Eleven Plus Exams

- 11+ Essentials - 3-D Non-verbal Reasoning Book 1 (First Past the Post) - CEM (Durham University)

- 11+ Essentials: 3D Diagrams, Non-Verbal Reasoning - Essential Practice Papers (First Past the Post) by Educational Experts (2013)

Publisher: The Armadillo's Pillow Ltd

- The Big 11+ Logic Puzzle Challenge

Publisher: Letts

- 11+ Non-Verbal Reasoning Flashcards (Letts 11+ Success)
- 11+ Non-Verbal Reasoning Quick Practice Tests Age 10-11 for the CEM Assessment tests (Letts 11+ Success)

Practice papers

Recommended practice papers are available from the following publishers. From the table below it becomes clear that these tests have a wide variation in difficulty. Publishers often suggest that your child needs to be scoring 75%+ in order to feel reasonably confident that they will gain a place. For Gloucestershire at least, our results do not bear this out.

Papers (in order of difficulty)

Publisher	Paper	Pass Score Range	Min. aim
Moon	11+ Practice Papers	60-85%*	65
Practice and Pass	Practice Tests	52-72%	56
Eureka	11+ Confidence	55-75%*	62
Letts	Get Started	50-88%	60
Letts	Get Ready	56-90%	70
CGP	Practice Tests	45-85%	71
Letts	Get Ahead	52-76%	62
Bond	Practice Papers	30-80%	52

*Letts, CGP and Bond are the most reliable publishers from our experience, but if you wish to do more tests, Moon and Eureka are the correct type of paper.

Recommended Order:

1) Letts	Get Started
2) Practice and Pass	Pack 1
3) Practice and Pass	Pack 2
4) CGP	Pack1
5) Letts	Get Ready
6) CGP	Pack 2/3
7) Bond	Pack 1 and 2
8) Letts	Get Ahead

Scores can improve significantly (up to 30%), with practice

Websites

Primary Maths Challenge (http://www.primarymathschallenge.org.uk/)

Free Rice (https://freerice.com/)

TES (https://www.tes.com/)

Mathsphere (http://www.mathsphere.co.uk/)

Cotswold Education (https://www.cotswoldeducation.co.uk/)

BBC Learning and BBC Bitesize (https://www.bbc.co.uk/bitesize)

Woodlands Junior (http://www.primaryhomeworkhelp.co.uk/)

Bond online (https://www.bond11plus.co.uk/)

IXL (for Years 5 and 6) (https://uk.ixl.com/)

11+ Exams (https://www.elevenplusexams.co.uk/)

Word List

abacus	a counting tool
abandon	leave
abhorrent	dreadful
abide	accept
abolish	get rid of
abrupt	sudden
absent	away
absolute	total
abstain	to deliberately not be involved with something
absurd	ridiculous
abundance	plenty
accelerate	become faster
accomplishment	achievement
achieve	succeed
acquire	receive
acquisition	something received
acute	an angle of less than 90 degrees
admire	be impressed with
adopt	take on/change
adroit	quick and skilful
adversity	difficulty
advocate	supporting representative/recommend
affluent	wealthy
agile	nimble, can move with ease
agitated	annoyed
aid	help
ajar	slightly open
alarmed	suddenly concerned
albatross	a large sea bird
alder	a tree
alighted	left by taking a step down i.e. alighted the bus
alter	change
amaryllis	a flower
amass	collect
amber	an orange/brown colours. Also, a type of fossil
ambush	attack from a hidden place
amethyst	a clear purple stone
amiable	friendly and easy going
amicable	friendly
amorous	romantic

amphibian	animal that can live on land or in the water
amulet	a lucky charm or object
ancestor	someone genetically related from the distant past
anchor	a heavy hook used to stabilise
angel	a heavenly being
angle	the difference in direction between two touching lines
annihilate	completely destroy
ante (root)	before
anthology	a collection of writings by different authors in a single book
anti (root)	against
anvil	a heavy iron block
anxious	worried
ape	copy/joke
appalled	disgusted
arch	a curved line
archaeologist	a person that studies the past by examining objects
architect	a person that designs and builds
arid	dry
armoire	a cabinet
arsenal	a collection of guns
artificial	fake, unnatural
ascend	go up
ash	a type of tree
aspect	a view
assemble	join together
assist	help
assistance	to provide help
aster	a type of tree
astute	very intelligent and aware
attempt	try
aubergine	a dark purple vegetable
audio	sound
aural	related to the sense of hearing
auspicious	promising/favourable
aviary	a large cage used to keep birds
avoid	keep away from
awe	amazement
awning	material attached to a caravan or tent for extra cover
axes	more than one axe- a wood cutting tool
axis	a line used to show position
azalea	a flower
azure	a bright blue

Babbage	Recognised as the inventor of the computer
badger	pester/ a mammal
baffle	confused
baguette	a long stick of bread - French
baking	heat at a high temperature
bald	without hair (usually referring to the head)
balmy	hot
barber	a hairdresser for men
barometer	an instrument to measure pressure
barrel	a large container for liquid
barrister	a lawyer that works in a high court
base	bottom
based	where a personal is centrally located
bashful	shy
bass	a fish/ A type of guitar
bassoon	a large woodwind instrument
baste	pour hot fat over meat whilst cooking
bawled	the way a baby cried loudly
baying	demanding
beach	a sandy place near the sea
beaming	smiling/letting out rays
beech	a type of tree
begonia	a flower
ben (root)	good
beneficial	positive
benefit	an advantage
benign	harmless
bereft	missing
beret	a felt hat, traditionally French
besieged	overtaken completely
betrayal	a disloyal behaviour
bewildered	confused
bi (root)	two
bilingual	a person that can speak two languages fluently
bio (root)	earth
birch	a type of tree
biting	chilly
bitter	very cold
blacklist	a list of names put there for a negative reason
blacksmith	a person who works with metal to create or repair
blank	empty
bleak	dull, dismal

bloated	swollen, enlarged
blonde	a light-yellow colour
blush (colour)	a pink/red colour
blustery	very windy
boar	a male pig
boast	to show off
bolster	to support
bore	dull
boundary	edge/perimeter
buoyant	positive/able to float
bovine	cattle
bow	a hair tie/ben the body at the waist/front of a ship
Braille	Louis Braille invented a form of writing for the blind - braille
breath	air inhaled and exhaled
brilliant	clever/bright
broach	introduce, bring up a subject
brogue	a type of leather shoe
brooch	jewellery worn with a pin to hold it in place
brood	a collection of hens or children/to think for a long time in a negative way
brunette	dark brown
bulbous	large and round
bulky	difficult to carry due to shape
bunting	row of small flags on a string
burden	something difficult to manage
burdensome	difficult to manage
burgundy	deep red
buzzard	a bird of prey
cabana	a tent used as a dressing room by the sea
cackle	a wicked laugh
cacophony	a loud collection of noises
cajole	persuade
callous	cruel
callus	a thick unwanted piece of skin
camouflage	covering used to hid by blending into the background
candidly	honestly
canine	dog
canny	clever
cantankerous	bad-tempered
cantering	speed of horse between trot and gallop
capable	able
capacity	ability to do something/the amount held in total
carbon	a chemical element

cargo	a load carried by land or air
caricatures	a drawing or picture of someone with exaggerated features
carnation	a flower
carpenter	a person that uses wood to make or repair things
cartographer	a person who makes maps
cassette	a container that holds recorded music
castanets	percussion instrument used in the hands
casual	relaxed, informal
catalogue	a list of a collection of similar things
cease	stop/end
cellar	basement
cent	small unit worth one hundredth of a dollar
century	100 years
chaos	mayhem
chaotic	disorganised
chaperone	person that watches and protects another
charge	blame/provide power/payment/move forward/responsibility
charmed	persuaded by attractive qualities
chartreuse	a green/yellow colour
chasm	a large gap
chastise	scold
chatter	talk (usually quick conversation)
cherish	care greatly
chevron	An ^ symbol
chief	lead
chilly	cold
chisel	small tool for shaping
choir	a singing group
chord	more than one musical note played at a time
chromo (root)	colour
chrysanthemum	a flower
chute	a long tube/passage
civil	official status in a town or city
clarify	make clear
clarinet	woodwind instrument
cleaver	a large axe like tool
clement	pleasant
cloak	cover
close	near/not open/stifling
coarse	rough
coax	persuade
cogitate	think deeply

colonel	army rank - officer
combine	mix/join
commence	begin/start
commend	praise
compass	instrument for measuring direction
complete	total/all
complicate	make difficult
comprehend	understand
comprehensible	understandable
comprehensive	complete
conceal	hide
conceited	vain
condemn	blame
condiment	items such as salt, pepper and mustard that can enhance flavour by adding at the table
confidential	private
confound	completely surprise to the point that opinions may change
confront	stand up to
consideration	serious thought
constable	police officer
constant	unchanging
contact	touch
contemporary	now/modern/up-to date
contract	become less
contradict	the opposite
conundrum	a hard puzzle
convenient	easily usable
convent	a nun's home
copse	a small collection of trees
copyright	the ability/or not to copy original works
cord	string/rope
cordial	friendly/a soft drink
cornet	a brass instrument
courtesy	politeness
coy	shy
crane	a lifting vehicle/a wading bird
cranium	brain
cranky	grumpy
cravat	a piece of cloth worn around the neck - similar to a tie
craving	desire
create	design and make
creek	a small stream

criminal	wrong doing/wrong doer
crisp	a sound used to describe the crunching of snow or a bright, frosty day
crochet	a type of knitting
crocus	a flower
crucial	essential/necessary
cue	prompt
cuff links	jewellery used to tie together buttonholes on shirt cuffs
culottes	calf length, wide leg trousers
cunning	cleverness
Curie	A French scientist - Marie Curie
curiosity	interest
cursed	received an evil spell
cymbal	a percussion instrument
dahlia	a flower
dam	a device to stop the flow of water and change water level
dank	wet and unpleasant
Darwin	Charles Darwin put forward the Theory of Evolution
DaVinci	Leonardo DaVinci - famous painter, sculptor and inventor
dawn	beginning of daylight on a day
dearth	lack
debate	a formal discussion
debrief	a report about an activity that has taken place
decade	ten years
decay	fall into ruin
deceased	dead
deceitful	untrustworthy
deceive	mislead/lie
deceptive	misleading
decimate	totally destroy
decline	turn down/downward direction
decorated	awarded/embellished
defect	mistake/change nationality
defile	ruin
deflated	make less/disappoint
defy	act against
dejected	feel unappreciated
delayed	late
deliberation	serious consideration
delphinium	a flower
delusion	fantasy/ridiculous belief
demolish	destroy
dense	thick

desert	large area of very dry land/leave without permission
despair	sadness that feels it will be unending
despise	hate
despondent	sad
despot	tyrannical leader
detect	discover
device	instrument
devise	creating a plan or way of doing something
dexterity	ability to use hands well
dictator	a ruler with no opposition
dietician	healthy eating expert
dilapidated	broken/ramshackle (usually of a house)
diluted	made less pure
din	a loud noise
dinghy	a small boat
diplomatic	careful not to offend
dire	dreadful
discus	a disc thrown in an athletics sport
discuss	talk about
disfigure	maim/ruin/change
dishevelled	messy/untidy
dismal	dull/dreary
disobey	break the rules
dispute	argument
dissipate	become less
distinct	clear/unique
distraught	desperately upset
donation	gift
dozen	twelve
draughty	places where air escapes and cools an area
dramatic	very noticeable
draper	shop keeper who sells cloth
dreary	dull/dismal
drenched	very wet
dribbling	footballer jogging with the ball/saliva escaping from the mouth
drizzle	light rain
dual	two
duel	a fight between two people (historic)
dusk	the time that the sun goes down
dwelling	living space
dwindle	become fewer
easel	apparatus to hold canvas whilst a picture is being painted

ebony	black
economical	careful with money
economy	relates to money
Edison	Thomas Edison - invented the electric light bulb
effort	determination
Eire	Ireland (Irish term)
elderly	older people
elegant	pleasing and graceful
elephantine	related to elephant
elevated	raised
elliptical	oval
embark	set off (usually on a journey)
embarrassment	shame/humiliation
embezzled	stolen (money)
emerald	green
emulsion	a type of paint
enable	allow
enchanting	magical
enclosure	fence
encyclopaedia	book(s) of facts on many subjects
endanger	make unsafe
endure	cope with
engineer	a designer and builder of engines
engulf	take over
enigma	puzzle
enlighten	become aware
entire	total
equator	imaginary line around the centre of the globe
equine	related to horses
erratic	unstable
errand	a short journey for a particular purpose
escalated	rose up
escorted	led
essay	a written composition
estate agent	a seller of houses
esteem	regard for someone
estuary	small waterway at the mouth of a river
ewe	female sheep
exasperated	extremely frustrated
excessive	too much
exhale	breath out
exhaustive	entire amount

exhilarating	very exciting
exorbitant	very expensive
expand	become bigger
expel	let go
expenditure	money spent
exploit	an adventure/to take advantage of
exposed	shown
exquisite	very beautiful
exterior	outside
extinct	never to live again
extract	a part
extravagant	a fancy or expensive
fabrication	a lie
faint	light in colour/to lose consciousness for a time
fallow	left bare
falter	fall
familiar	recognisable
famished	very hungry
farrier	a person that provides shoes for horses
fathom	a measure of depth/understand
favour	prefer
feeble	weak
feet	an achievement/ plural of foot/twelve inches
feline	cat
fern	plant with a long stem and feathery leaves
fickle	easily changes sides
fiction	imaginative writing
financial	regarding money
finch	a bird
fir	a type of tree
flawless	without error/perfect
flax	a plant with blue flowers
flea	a very small insect
flee	leave quickly
flint	grey/black stone - often used to make tools
flippant	trivial, unthinking
florist	a flower seller
flotilla	a collection of ships
focus	central/pay attention
foe	enemy
foil	a metallic sheet/to uncover a scheme
foliage	leaves of a plant

ford	shallow part of a river
forceps	instrument used by a doctor
forgo	do without
fort	a strong build that keeps soldiers safe
fortuitous	lucky
fortunate	lucky
foul	putrid/wrong doing
foundry	factory
foundation	base/bottom
fourth	between third and fifth
fowl	bird
frail	weak
frame	edge
freesia	a flower
freezing	icy
frequent	often
fret	worry
frigid	very cold
furious	very angry
futile	useless
futon	a couch than can transform into a bed
gait	a way of walking
Galileo	Galileo - known as the Father of Science
gallant	brave
galoshes	rubber shoes to wear in a wet place
gamut	the complete range
gargantuan	huge
garnet (colour)	dep red
gather	come together
gauntlet	a strong glove
gavel	the 'hammer' used by a judge in court
gem	precious stone
genes	cells passed down through generations
gent	informal form of gentleman
geo (root)	earth
geranium	a flower
gifted	talented/prodigy
gingerly	carefully
glacial	related to the presence of ice
gladiolus	a flower
glazier	a person that works with glass/windows
gloomy	dull

gluttony	greediness
gown	dress
granite	very hard rock/dark grey
graphite (colour)	dark grey
grasp	understand/hold tight
grey	between black and white
grieve	mourn - sorrow following a death
grimace	a negative expression on the face
gripe	complaint
grotesque	ugly
grouse	wild fowl - bird
guerrilla	a small group that fights together for a cause
guillotine	instrument used to behead people
guise	image
gullible	too trusting of others
gusty	very windy
Gutenberg	Gutenberg - inventor of the printing press
haberdashery	in relation to sewing
haddock	a fish
hamper	hinder/block
hapless	unlucky, unfortunate
harp	a sting instrument/to talk incessantly about something
hastily	quickly
haughty	arrogant
Hawking	Stephen Hawking - Author of 'A Brief History of Time'
hawthorn	a type of tree
hazel	a type of tree
hazy	unclear/foggy
heir	person in line to receive an estate or other fortune
helix	a spiral
hemp	plant used for making rope
heron	a bird
hesitate	pause/delay action
hibiscus	a flower
hinder	block/get in the way
hinge	a device used to join two things together - especially a door to a frame
hoarse	a rough voice (usually with a sore throat)
hoax	an untruth set out as a truth
honest	truthful
horde	crowd/large amount
horizon	line in the distance where the sky appears to meet the land or sea
horn-rimmed	glasses with plastic frames that appear to look like horn was used

host	collection of angels/television presenter
hostile	unfriendly
hub	centre
humble	modest
humid	hot and wet
hydrangea	a flower
hyena	wild dog
hype (root)	over
hypo (root)	under
icy	freezing/zero degrees Celsius or below
ignite	light
ignore	take no notice of
immature	childish/not grown
immense	childish/not grown
imp	small, devilish creature
impair	weaken/damage
impatient	unprepared to wait
impertinent	rude
imply	suggest
import	bring into a country
impoverished	very poor
impure	mixed
incessantly	continuing
incision	cut
inclement	unpleasant
incognito	disguised
index	first finger/list of names
indifferent	uncaring
indignant	shocked and angry about a perceived unfairness
indigo	a purple
indispensable	necessary
indistinct	unclear
indolent	lazy
indulge	treat
industrious	hard working
inept	incapable
infantile	immature
inferno	a large fire
influence	persuade
inheritance	fortune received from a person upon their death
inoculate	vaccinate/make safe
inquire	ask

inscribe	writing that is carved
intercept	go between
internal	inside
interrogate	ask in a harsh way
intersection	joining place/crossover
interval	break
intrigue	arouse curiosity
irate	furious
iris	part of the eye
irritated	frustrated
jagged	rough and uneven with sharp, pointed edges
jasmine	a climbing, flowering plant
jeer	laugh unkindly
jester	joker/wit
John Doe	a person who is unknown by name
jovial	happy
juniper	an evergreen bush
kernel	the inside of a nut
kidney	an organ in the body
kin	relative/family
kindle	set a fire/begin to feel an emotion
knave	a dishonest person
knead	press and squeeze/massage
knit	tie other (often wool)
knot	tie tightly/a measure of nautical speed
labyrinth	a maze
lack	be without
lair	an animal home/a trap
lance	a pole weapon/to cut open
lap	top of the legs when sitting/a circuit
larder	pantry/storage place for food
lark	a bird
larkspur	a flower
latitude	imaginary horizontal lines around the globe used to assist with locating places
launch	throw/pitch/begin
lax	casual/not careful
leaf	part of a tree/page of a book
leak	an escape of liquid
least	the smallest amount
leek	a vegetable from the onion family
leisure	relaxation

leisurely	calmly/acting with ease
lens	transparent material that alters the direction of light
leotard	stretchy clothing used by dancers and for exercise
lethargic	very tired
liable	responsible
lieutenant	officer rank in the army
lilac	a light purple
limb	arm, leg or wing
limit	maximum or minimum amount
linguist	a person that can speak several languages fluently
lithe	a person that can move quickly and easily
litter	rubbish
liver	an organ in the body
livid	very angry
lobe	a low hanging part, especially of an ear
locket	a small ornamental case often worn around the neck on a string
lodge	a dwelling
lofty	tall
logo (root)	word/reason
loyalty	a strong feeling of support
lucid	clear speech
luke warm	a mild warm temperature
luminous	giving off light/bright or shiny
lute	a string instrument
luxurious	expensive, comfortable and elegant
mace	a club like weapon
mahogany	deep red colour
maim	harm
maize	plant that produces sweet corn
major	of great importance
mal (root)	bad
malady	illness/disease
malice	nastiness/cruelty
malicious	unkind
manor	a grand home
manse	a home for a priest
martyr	a person that dies for a cause that they believe in
mask	cover
matted	tangled into a thick mess
mauve	light purple
meander	bends/twists
menacing	threatening

mentality	a way of thinking
meteorologist	a weather expert
methodical	orderly
micro (root)	very small
millennium	one thousand years
milliner	make and sells hats
mimic	copy
miner	a digger (often of coal or gold)
mingle	mix
minor	lesser
minority	the least
minute	sixty seconds/very small
mirth	amusement and laughter
mischief	naughtiness
misty	foggy/cloudy
modern	up-to-date/new/contemporary
modest	humble
modify	change
moisture	wet
mono (root)	one thousand years
morph	change
Morse	Morse - creator of a message system of dots and dashes
motivate	encourage
mourning	a time of grief following the death of a loved one
muggy	dense/foggy
mulberry	a purple/brown colour and a type of bush
mumble	to speak in an unclear way
murder	to intentionally kill someone/a group of crows
murky	thick/unclear
nadir	the lowest point
narcissus	a flower
nauseous	sickly
navy	dark blue
nebulous	foggy
neon	chemical element/fluorescent light/an extremely bright colour
Newton	Sir Isaac Newton - explained gravity to us
nib	tip of a pen that distributes the ink
nimble	agile
nippy	chilly
noble	showing fine qualities/rank arrived at by being born into the aristocracy (especially in medieval England)
noncommittal	not expressing an opinion

nonentity	of no worth or identity
notice	become aware/see/a sign
novel	new or unusual/a written story
novice	beginner
nullify	become nothing
nylon	a synthetic material
oak	a type of tree
oasis	a small area in a desert where there is water and plants grow
oath	a promise
obscure	little seen or known
obtain	receive
obvious	clear
ominous	threatening
omit	leave out
opaque	non see-through
opponent	rival/enemy
oppressive	harsh
optimal	most/best
optimistic	positive feeling
oral	spoken not written
orca	a type of whale (killer)
orchid	a flower
originate	begin
orthodontist	an expert that can reposition teeth
ostentatious	showy/over-the-top
oust	get rid of
overalls	a piece of clothing covering legs and torso
overcast	cloudy
pachyderm	a large animal with thick skin
pack	a collection of wolves/put together in one place/a bag
palindrome	a word that reads the same when spelt forwards or backwards
palm	a tree/flat part of a hand
pansy	a flower
papyrus	plant based material that the ancient Egyptians used to write on
paramedic	ambulance worker
paramount	of most importance
parched	dry/thirsty
parchment	during writing material - often used in medieval times
parliament	meeting place of a country's law-makers/a collection of owls
parlour	larder/food storage place
parsley	a herb
partridge	a bird - wild fowl

passive	not involved
Pasteur	Louis Pasteur - scientist responsible for pasteurising process (milk safety)
patch	fix or mend/small cover
patience	willingness to wait
patient	a person requiring assistance (hospital), being capable of waiting
patriot	a personal that is a great supporter of their country
patter	a repeated light, tapping sound
peak	a very top
pedagogue	a teacher - especially a very strict one
pedestrian	a walker/normal-not exciting
pendant	a piece of jewellery usually worn around the neck
penetrate	to go into
peony	a flower
periphery	the outside edge
perilous	dangerous
perimeter	fence/edge
perish	die
periwinkle	purple/blue colour
permit	allow/a ticket that gives permission
perpetuate	continue and enforce
perplexed	puzzled
persevere	to keep trying
perspiring	sweating
perturbed	bothered/worried
pestered	bothered - not left alone
petroleum	a fuel
pewter (colour)	dark grey
pharmacist	chemist
phobia	fear
phone (sound)	sound
photo (root)	light
physician	doctor
piccolo	a small flute
piercing	a small, sharp hole or sound
pigment	colour
pine	a tree/to miss someone or something
pipette	a small tube for transferring liquid
pique	a feeling of annoyance
pirouette	to turn in a single place
piscine	of fish
pitch	throw/a sports field/the quality of a sound
pitcher	a jug/a person throwing/put forward

placid	calm
plaice	a fish
pleasant	enjoyable
pliable	flexible/bendy
pliers	a grasping tool
plover	a wading bird
plumber	a person that fixes water pipes
plume	a long cloud of smoke or feathers spread out
plunder	stolen goods/the stealing of goods
pod	a collection of whales/where peas are found
polar	relating to the north or south poles
poly (root)	many
poinsettia	a flower
porter	a person paid to carry luggage and other loads
post	after
postpone	leave until later
praise	compliment
precipitation	rain, sleet or snow
predicament	problematic situation
priceless	no value
pride	a collection of lions/a feeling of worth
primary	main/basic/central
prime	a number divisible only by one and itself/central
principal	lead
principle	moral
prodigy	highly gifted and talented
progress	move forward
progression	the act of moving forward/improving
prohibit	not allow/stop
promote	encourage/actively support
protrude	stick out
prudence	cautiousness
pseudo	fake/pretend
public	about the whole/common/widespread
pulsate	beat
pulverize	to beat/destroy
pungent	a strong smell
puzzled	confused
qualm	unease
quantity	amount
quartz	a hard (usually colourless) mineral
quay	a long structure used to tie boats

query	question
queue	a line for orderly waiting
quiver	shake/a collection of arrows
rabble	mob/an unruly group of people
radiant	bright/shiny
raging	angry
raiment	clothing, fabric
ramble	walk - usually in the countryside
rare	uncommon
rate	a measurement (of speed), a charge, a given standard
ravenous	very hungry
raw	uncooked/a feeling of sensitivity
re-establish	to make important again
rebuke	scold
receptionist	a person who greets visitors at work
rectified	fixed
reel	a cylinder for winding thread around/winding
reform	make a positive change
refrain	to stop doing
regard	care for/look at
regression	become worse
reign	time spent ruling (kings and queens)
reject	turn down
relate	connect
release	let go
reliable	trustworthy
renovate	to fix and improve
renowned	well known
replica	a copy
replicate	to copy
resemble	look like
residence	a living place
restrict	limit
reveal	show
revulsion	disgust
rhododendron	a flower
rigid	inflexible/cannot be bent
roast	to heat for a long time
robust	strong and sturdy
rogue	unlawful/behave badly
role	part played/position
rota	a list of names giving an order for events

rough	uneven/craggy/not gentle
rupture	tear
rural	not of the town - countryside
rye	a cereal plant
sabotage	deliberately ruin
sack	a back/loss of a job
salamander	an amphibian
saline	salt
salvation	being saved
sanctuary	a safe place
sanguine	cheerful
sapless	weak/lacking bodily strength
sapphire	a gem/deep blue colour
saturated	completely filled (with water usually)
scalpel	an instrument a doctor uses - a cutting blade
scene	a picture/view
scent	something than can be smelt
scholar	a highly educated person
scoff	to laugh in a cruel way
scold	to chastise/tell off
scope (root)	see
scorch	to burn
scrawny	thin and bony
scruffy	untidy
scythe	a tool used of cutting crops
sear	to burn
secure	make safe
seize	to take possession of
seldom	rarely/not often
serenade	to sing romantically
serenity	peace
sermon	a speech about religion or another moral subject
sett	a badger's home
sever	to tear apart
several	more than a few but less than many
severe	serious
shabby	old and untidy
sham	fake
shambles	a mess
shape	the outside form of something
shawl	a large scarf
shelter	a place of safety

shifty	suspicious looking
shotput	an athletics sport that involves throwing a very heavy ball
shrivelled	has become smaller and is wrinkly
shroud	cover
Siberian	related to Siberia
sceptical	untrusting
sketch	drawing
skimmed	go over quickly/remove cover from a liquid surface
slander	to speak unfairly about someone
slate	a collection of candidates/dark grey hard stone
sleek	smooth and glossy
sleet	between rain and snow
slovenly	lazily
slumber	sleep
smog	a dirty, smoky fog
snapdragon	a flower
snooty	self-important
solace	comfort during a sad time
solemn	serious
solid	firm/sturdy
sombrero	a wide-brimmed hat
sopping	very wet
soprano	singer of high musical notes
sound	solid/a noise
sovereign	ruler (king or queen)
sow	female pig/plant seeds
spectacles	glasses
spectrum	the entire range
sphere	ball
spirit level	an instrument for measure the horizontal level of something
spruce	a tree/make neat, fresh and tidy
spy	notice/see
squabble	argue in a small way
squander	loss through carelessness
stable	sturdy/a place that provides animal shelter
stallion	male horse
static	still
steadfast	steady
stethoscope	a doctor's hearing instrument
stifling	hot and uncomfortable
stiletto	a shoe with a long, sharp heel
stimulate	excite

stonemason	a person that carves and builds with stone
strife	war/fighting
strut	a confident walk
sturdy	firm, steady
sub (root)	under
subdued	quiet
subsequent	next
subsidiary	a less important part of a whole
succeed	achieve
successor	the person or thing that comes after
suede	the soft inside of leather material
sugar-coat	make something appear better than it actually is
sullen	grumpy
sultry	hot and humid
summit	the very top/apex
surplus	extra
suspicion	wariness
suspicious	appearing to be wrong
swallow	a bird/food or drink passing down the throat
sweltering	very hot
swift	a bird/fast
swindle	cheat
swollen	enlarged
symbol	a mark with a particular meaning
syn (root)	same
syringe	a small pump
tablet	flat slab of stone/a pill/small portable computer
taboo	something not talked about as doing so is considered improper
tact	a polite and kind way of talking
tailor	a person that makes fitted clothes/to shape purposefully
talon	a bird's claw
tangerine	an orange colour
tardy	late
tartan	a checkered fabric
tawny (colour)	brown
teak	a type of tree/wood
teal	a duck/greenish-blue colour
temperate	mild
tempestuous	angry
template	example/a shape used to create patterns
temporary	not forever
tepee	a conical (cone shaped) tent

tepid	slightly warm
textile	material
theatre	a place where plays are performed
threatened	endangered
thrilling	exciting
timpani	kettle drums
toil	work
tolerate	endure
torrential	very heavy (rain)
torment	tease/deliberately cause difficulty
torque	a force that causes rotation
trance	in a dream' but awake
tranquil	peaceful
trawler	a type of ship
treacherous	dangerous
trial	test
triangle	a shape with three sides and three corners
tribe	group
trickle	a small amount of dripping liquid
trilby	a type of hat
trivial	of little importance
trotter	a pig's foot
trove	store of valuable things
tuba	a brass instrument
turbulent	unsettled/chaotic
tutor	private teacher
tuxedo	a suit with a dinner jacket and a bow tie
thwart	prevent something from happening
twilight	semi-darkness when the sun is just below the horizon
umpire	referee
uncredited	given no value
undertaker	the person that arranges funerals and burials
unearth	discover
uni (root)	one
unidentified	unknown/nor recognized
university	a large educational establishment
unkempt	untidy/messy
unravel	become undone
unruly	disorderly
upholstery	furniture
urn	vase
vague	unclear

vain	having a high opinion of one's own appearance
vane	instrument for gauging wind direction
vat	a large tank for holding liquid
vein	small tubes in the body that carry blood
ventilator	a device that blows air
vice	poor habit/second/gripping tool
vigilance	awareness/watchfulness
viscose	a smooth material that feels similar to silk
volatile	unstable - likely to erupt
voluntary	by choice
waddle	walk with short, clumsy steps
walnut	a nut
warp	bend/twist
warren	rabbit's home
weary	tired
whetted	sharpened blade
wholesome	healthy
willow	a type of tree
windswept	carried by the wind/untidy/unkempt
wing-back	a type of armchair
x-ray	machine for photographing parts of the body
yew	a type of tree
yield	give way/accept
yoke	a collar/harness
yolk	the yellow part of an egg
zeal	great energy and enthusiasm
zenith	the highest point

About the Authors

Ian Todd BSc (Hons), PGCert HE, PhD has worked in the education and research sector all his life. He is the founder of Cotswold Education and is a retired academic. He was Head of Biology at Bath Spa University for 14 years and previously Senior Lecturer at the University of Hertfordshire. He has extensive research experience at Oxford University and Cambridge University having obtained a PhD and BSc (Hons) from Cardiff University. Ian has also personally tutored for many years and his media appearances include BBC1 One Show and BBC Radio Gloucestershire.

Liz Fortson BEd (Hons) has also been a life-long educator. She taught in the primary sector for ten years; becoming a departmental Head of English and Primary Lead teacher.

Upon marrying, Liz moved to America where she taught in Gifted and Talented programme classrooms and Special Needs. Since returning to the UK she has tutored many children for the 11+ Exam in Gloucestershire over the past nine years.

Printed in Great Britain
by Amazon